Better Writing

Beyond Periods and Commas

Travis Koll

ROWMAN & LITTLEFIELD EDUCATION
A division of
ROWMAN & LITTLEFIELD PUBLISHERS, INC.
Lanham • New York • Toronto • Plymouth, UK

This book was placed by the Educational Design Services LLC literary agency.

Published by Rowman & Littlefield Education
A division of Rowman & Littlefield Publishers, Inc.
A wholly owned subsidary of The Rowman & Littlefield Publishing Group, Inc.
4501 Forbes Boulevard, Suite 200, Lanham, Maryland 20706
www.rowman.com

10 Thornbury Road, Plymouth PL6 7PP, United Kingdom

British Library Cataloguing in Publication Information Available

Library of Congress Cataloging-in-Publication Data

Koll, Travis, 1978–
Better writing : beyond periods and commas / Travis Koll.
p. cm.
ISBN 978-1-61048-587-6 (cloth : alk. paper) — ISBN 978-1-61048-588-3 (pbk. : alk. paper) —
ISBN 978-1-61048-589-0 (electronic)
1. English language—Rhetoric. 2. Report writing. 3. Persuasion (Rhetoric) 4. Creative writing. I.
Title.
PE1408.K695 2012
808'.042—dc23
2012001298

Printed in the United States of America

For Grandma

Contents

Preface

The intention behind this book is a simple one: provide students and the general public with a straightforward and unpretentious guide to better writing. To that end, *Better Writing: Beyond Periods and Commas* encourages novice writers to adopt a holistic and creative approach to composition rather than obsessing about rules and templates and lists of "dos" and "don'ts." In doing so, it drives would-be writers to actively and consciously participate in the composition process, helping them better understand the strategies, conventions, and joys found in good writing.

It's definitively understandable that some teachers, professors, and administrators accustomed to enormous writing manuals may wonder how such a compact and concise book can accomplish this. Indeed, those gigantic textbooks certainly offer more content and provide exhaustive explanations of every possible rhetorical situation a student may encounter.

Of course, that's often part of the problem. Imagine how the average composition student—filled with anxiety, confusion, and perhaps even outright disdain for writing—probably feels when confronted with such a tome of instruction. Does he or she sigh with relief, glad to at last have hundreds of pages that explain every detail of every writing task imaginable? Or does he or she feel overwhelmed and intimidated by so much information, so many possibilities, and so many pages of text, all seemingly suggesting that writing well is just too difficult?

In my experience, the latter is more likely true.

At its core, this book is simply a conversation that I believe many composition teachers and instructors would like to have with their students: a casual and, at times, personal discussion about what it *really* means to write well.

If you're an educator, I encourage you to use it as such. Allow the topics examined herein to serve as catalysts for your own conversations; use the chapters and exercises to help students move beyond the false belief that writing is just about grammar and punctuation. Also encourage your novice writers to recognize and use strategy and creativity in their own works.

If you're a student or just someone looking to improve your writing skills, use this book as a tool for developing your potential. As I suggest many times in the following pages, writing is a tremendously significant expression of what it means to be human. You can indeed better your abilities through practice and study.

One final note: The language and tone of this book are very informal and straightforward, but nothing in its style or content should be taken as disrespectful. In fact, the casual and honest language is a testament to my deeply held admiration for students and novice writers, especially those courageous enough to confront their difficulties with writing head-on. In my opinion, students and writers deserve such honesty, as only a genuine (and occasionally humorous) look at the subject will lead to real understanding and improvement.

Acknowledgments

I would first like to thank my agent, Bertram Linder of Educational Design Services, LLC, for all his work toward the success of this project. I must also extend my sincere gratitude to Tom Koerner and the staff of Rowman & Littlefield Education for helping to bring this book to the market.

Finally, and most importantly, I would like to thank my wife, Tammy, and my son, Jonathan, for always supporting me and my writing. I love you both.

Introduction

THE TEACHER'S PERSPECTIVE

If you were to step into any college English instructor's office on a typical day, you'd likely find the following: an aging computer sitting atop an aging desk, walls adorned with pictures of dead authors and profound-sounding quotes, a black filing cabinet filled with five years' worth of old essays and attendance sheets, and a small bookcase stuffed with texts by Shakespeare and Milton, Dickens and Eliot. You know the ones: the novels and poems and plays that only English teachers seem to like.

You'd also likely find him or her sitting there, stooped over a fresh stack of papers, exhausted and frustrated and yet still filled with hope that the next essay he or she reads will display the skill and passion that hides somewhere within every student and every writer.

Despite what they may say in class, few are really looking for stunning talent or genius in an essay; they're certainly not searching for fireworks or explosions or the next great American author. In fact, many are not even especially interested in your grammar and punctuation skills, at least not beyond your ability to write a sentence they can understand—the sort that doesn't give rise to an immediate headache.

Truthfully, what many are really hoping to see is pretty simple: that you've been paying attention in class; that you have the capacity and willingness to think and see beyond your own immediate world; that you can express yourself in a way others will understand and take seriously; and, ultimately, that you care about what you're doing.

Lots of papers fail to fulfill at least one of these hopes. For example, look at George's essay: Even though his class spent more than a week on the fundamentals of research and citations, you'd never know it to look at his work—no sign at all that he'd done any research or knows how to cite a source. It's all a collection of uncited quotes from random blogs and personal interviews with his uncle's best friend.

Equally frustrating, Ellen's paper told her teacher a story about her family's last trip to the coast. Unfortunately, she was supposed to craft an academic argument about an important social issue.

Happily, James's essay included strong research and citations, and he did indeed follow the assignment's instructions, but the text read more like an email to his buddy than a college paper. He even used Internet emoticons and webspeak throughout. LOL!!! ROTFL!!! It's unlikely that his instructor did either while reading his work.

Mia's essay ended up at the bottom of the pile. It looked as if she'd copied and pasted huge chunks of an article right off a website and didn't even bother to remove the banners and hyperlinks scattered through the text, or to change the text's 18-point font. Teachers don't really notice things like that, right? She and her teacher will talk very soon.

All of this may strike you as odd, especially if you've spent years diagramming sentences, searching for that all-too-important subject/predicate/pronoun/adverb/adjective so popular in grammar exercises. But there's one thing you must understand before we go any further: in all likelihood, your English and composition teachers, instructors, and professors *love* writing.

This isn't to say that they have passionate discussions about the newest trends in comma usage or argue endlessly about when it's appropriate to split an infinitive. Rather, they love what writing allows them, and you, to do and achieve.

For many teachers, the writing process is more than merely a means of expression or rote communication. It is instead a tool for discovery; a method for connecting with people, both living and dead; and an avenue for exploring the world, our society, our shared humanity, and the very *stuff* that makes each of us who we are.

It's hardly surprising that many teachers and professors, who are filled with such passion and quite aware of writing's beauty and potential, are appalled when students fail to meet page requirements or express such disdain at the thought of putting a few words down on paper:

"I hate writing."
"Writing is a waste of time."
"I'm a terrible writer, and I always will be."

Alter these statements a bit and you can really see what they likely mean to your teachers and professors:

"I hate discovering new things about myself and the world. I just don't care about anything but myself, my own life, and my new phone."
"Connecting with my fellow human beings is a waste of time, even though I spend hours each day texting friends or posting on social networking sites."

"I never get good grades on essays, so I must have nothing worthwhile to say."

In truth, all students probably mean when they make such statements is that they don't understand writing, have never felt comfortable with it, and would rather mask those insecurities with an "I couldn't care less" façade. Of course, as illustrated above, that's not what teachers of writing usually perceive. Fair or not, it's the truth.

What matters is that novice writers recognize (1) that they likely don't hate writing so much as their insecurities or past experiences concerning it; (2) that writing, even when just creating an email, is never a waste of time; and (3) that the ability to write well isn't entirely dependent upon one's DNA.

While some people may have an easier time with writing, and while others may struggle quite a bit more, everyone can learn to become a better writer. Yes. That's right. *Everyone*. All it takes is finding a good guide, mustering the courage to confront and overcome those deep-seated anxieties, and finally developing a willingness to practice, fall down (intellectually, of course), and practice even more.

Of course, this doesn't mean that you can necessarily become the next Shakespeare or Dickinson—only that you *can* improve. And likely a good deal.

It's easy enough to ignore this philosophy, just as it is to ignore the advice presented in this book. If you've struggled with writing for most of your life, those many years of frustration have likely made you feel all but allergic to essays and English classes. Perhaps you've had your share of bad composition teachers, of condescending professors, of papers dripping in red ink and discouragements. You're not alone. Many students are so wounded by past writing experiences that they've nearly given up on themselves and the art form altogether.

If this sounds familiar, here's some good advice: Don't. Don't give up on yourself or the opportunities writing well can offer. Don't give up on your right to participate in society's important discussions. Don't allow fear or frustration to prevent you from experiencing a craft that has brought so many within humanity a great deal of joy and wisdom and connection.

Writing, whether it's a poem or a passionate letter or even an academic essay, can be one of the purest expressions of what it means to be a human being, and we should all approach it as such.

Do so when studying this book. Leave those insecurities behind, examine and explore writing with a fresh and open perspective, and really give these ideas and approaches a chance.

An important note before we get started: If you're a student, please remember that you should *always* write and complete your assignments according to your teacher's suggestions and requirements. After all, he or she is the one assessing and grading your writing, so use the approaches and techniques discussed in this book only as a supplement to your teacher's lessons and instructions—*never* as a replacement for them.

The same holds true for standardized tests, as they often have specific requirements and evaluation parameters that may contradict the suggestions in this book. This text offers *no* guarantee of better grades or improved test scores. It simply offers a different perspective of and an approach to writing that may help you improve your skills.

Agreed?

Good.

DISCUSSION QUESTIONS

1. Describe some of your past experiences with writing, English classes, or particular assignments. What have you struggled with in the past? What do you continue to struggle with now? Finally, how do you believe these experiences have influenced your perceptions of and beliefs about writing, if at all?
2. Form a small group with a few of your fellow students and discuss your responses to Discussion Question 1. Have any of you had similar experiences with writing and/or English classes? If you could go back and alter the way you've been taught about writing in the past, would you? If so, what specific changes would you make, and why?

IN-CLASS EXERCISE

Choose a topic you love, one about which you're very passionate, and then write a half-page explanation of it for your peers. The topic can be anything you like: sports, music, art, television, and so on. Rather than focusing on why you find this topic so appealing and important, concentrate instead on convincing your readers to agree with you. Why should they like or care about this topic as much as you do?

After you've finished, craft another half-page of writing in which you reflect on your experience while writing the above essay. Was this fairly easy to write or still difficult? How does it compare/contrast with your other writing experiences?

AT-HOME ASSIGNMENT

Write a one- to two-page personal narrative in which you explain and describe your experiences as a writer, from the earliest assignments you can remember to your performances on more recent tasks.

While you want to ensure your text is readable, don't focus too much on small mechanical issues. Instead, concentrate on including specific details and explaining these to your readers. Here's an example of how you might start off:

> My first memories of writing are from the third grade—specifically, the little writing contests I'd have with a friend sitting next to me. The stories had a lot to do with recent movies I'd seen or a giant, ship-swallowing octopus monster that always seemed to find its way into my writing. I knew very little about grammar or punctuation at that time, but it didn't matter. . . .

Chapter One

About Those Commas and Periods . . .

MONICA'S STORY

Monica, a university freshman, steps into her first day of college English filled with terror: absolute, all-consuming, running-from-a-knife-wielding-maniac-in-a-bad-horror-movie terror. Clutching her bag and struggling to conceal her fear beneath an apathetic expression, she takes a seat in the back as memories of past English classes and assignments flood her mind.

Staring for hours at a blank computer screen, consoling herself after receiving yet another F on an essay, fighting back tears as her high school teacher ranted about sloppy punctuation and dangling modifiers—all of those experiences seemed proof enough that she was a terrible writer and would always be such.

After all, she's spent years trying to understand punctuation and grammar, apparently without much success. Despite all that time and all those lessons, she has no idea how to identify a sentence fragment, how to use a semicolon, or how to define an adverb or an adjective. She still doesn't understand why teachers always circle her commas in red or insist she rearrange the words in her sentences.

Hoping to improve her grades, Monica even saw a writing tutor for several months, a snotty college sophomore who insisted grammar and punctuation were "easy" if she'd just study hard and concentrate. Desperate, Monica studied harder, focused on all things mechanical, checked and rechecked every paper for mistakes, and still ended up with an unsatisfactory grade every time.

Like many students who struggle with writing, Monica suffers from a basic misconception concerning composition: namely, the idea that writing is all about its mechanical elements, particularly punctuation and grammar. For many of you, these aspects represent the "basics" of writing, the skills you must first master before even thinking about content, structure, or specific rhetorical techniques. But here's the thing: if you look closely at professional writing, you'll notice that we supposed masters of punctuation and grammar purposefully break the rules all the time.

In fact, that last sentence did so by starting with a conjunction—the *but* at the beginning is a big no-no. Despite the rule, the rhythms and content of the sentences justified the conjunction, and so the *Universal and Official Punctuation and Grammar Handbook* (which doesn't exist, by the way) was ignored. You see, writing well isn't about following the rules; indeed, those rules can get in the way.

RULES, RULES . . .

If you sit and listen to many writing teachers talk about punctuation and grammar—as you undoubtedly have for several years—you might think that the "rules" of writing are both ancient and universal. Surely, such rules were established when the earliest humans began scrawling upon their cave walls. Unfortunately, this perception of mechanics, and the pseudohistory upon which it is founded, is entirely inaccurate. In fact, the development of punctuation and grammar in the English language has been (and still is, to some degree) quite dynamic.

Without going into too much detail about the true history of that development, which you'd likely find dull, it's best to simply state that the rules concerning punctuation, grammar, and even spelling in English were anything but universal for most of the language's history. One need only look at the works of history's literary geniuses to see this. Have you ever tried to read Old or Middle English?

Despite what to modern eyes appears to be a spelling and grammatical nightmare, such writing was and is profound, inspirational, and indeed immortal. You see, many (if not most) great writers throughout history regarded spelling and punctuation and grammar as tools, not shackles. As throngs of linguists and morphologists spent centuries arguing about an ever-changing litany of rules, writers from Chaucer to Eliot to Dickens to Plath wrote to explore and share with the world. When following the "rulebook" benefited their respective pieces, they did so; when the rulebook interfered with their individual stylistic tastes, it was ignored.

In short, great writers don't become great because they blindly obey grammar and punctuation rules; they are great because of what they have to say and how they go about saying it.

SO SPELLING, GRAMMAR, AND PUNCTUATION DON'T MATTER?

When first learning of this approach to mechanics, students (and indeed some writing instructors) invariably and erroneously conclude that this chapter is suggesting that developing skills in spelling, grammar, and punctuation is unnecessary. This misinter-

pretation is understandable, especially given the recent media spec-
ulation about the "DEATH OF GRAMMAR!!!" and similar nonsense; however, such a perception simply isn't accurate.

The mechanical aspects of writing are indeed important, as important as the screws and nails holding up our homes and class-
rooms, and developing the associated skills is a vital step on your
road to becoming a good writer. But focusing on these skills to the
exclusion of all the other aspects of writing (focus, structure, rhetorical strategies, etc.) is like spending all your money on a bucket
of beautiful nails for a new home and having nothing left over for
lumber, plumbing, wiring, or even the doors and windows. Like
those nails, mechanics are a means to an end in writing, not an end
in and of themselves.

Perhaps a sports analogy could clarify this for you fans out
there: Concentrating solely on mechanics is similar to a basketball
team only practicing dribbling and spending no time on passing,
strategy, or shooting baskets. It's definitely no way to build a
house, win a game, or write well.

And here's some good news: you don't have to master mechanics before moving on to the other, more interesting aspects of writing; indeed, students often seem to learn better if they dive right in
and simply practice all of those skills at the same time.

Put simply, stop spending all your time focusing on your
spelling, grammar, and punctuation when you're writing or revising a paper (unless, of course, your instructor demands otherwise),
and definitely stop thinking of yourself as a poor writer because
you have trouble with those skills.

IF YOU INSIST

Despite this big lesson on the true role of mechanics in good writing, some of you would be perturbed if this chapter didn't at least
give you a few tips on tackling your grammar and punctuation

difficulties. Realizing such, let's briefly cover a few of the most common errors in student papers—specifically, how to identify and correct them.

For a more exhaustive explanation of these concepts, explore the style books associated with your particular class or one of the modern grammar and punctuation manuals currently on the market.

Sentence Fragments

A sentence fragment is also called an "incomplete sentence," and they generally drive writing instructors crazy. There's no need to bore you with an explanation of clauses, subjects, or predicates. Instead, one simply needs to understand that a sentence fragment usually lacks either a (1) central noun (what or whom the sentence is about) or (2) a central verb (a primary action happening in the sentence). Here are two examples of fragments, each missing either a central noun or verb:

Went out to a great restaurant. (What or who is the sentence about?)
To celebrate their anniversary, the young couple. (The couple what?)

Obviously, both of these are incomplete thoughts, and therefore they are also incomplete sentences. To fix such errors, all we must do is insert the missing part:

Cathy's parents went out to a great restaurant.
To celebrate their anniversary, the young couple *took a vacation to the Bahamas.*

See the difference? Now, there are, of course, many other ways to create a sentence fragment, just as there are other methods of fixing them. In essence, however, these corrections all work to transform a partial thought (a "thought fragment") into a whole one. If you complete the thought, you complete the sentence.

Commas

It's a common complaint: commas confuse you, frustrate you, and indeed just generally tick you off. Here's a little secret—commas often have the same effect on writing instructors, especially when they are placed in a sentence solely on the basis of pausing or breathing.

Such errors aren't entirely your fault. Most writing instructors can probably still remember their own elementary school teachers telling them, "Whenever you pause or take a breath in a sentence, make sure to place a comma there." Such advice has resulted in the rather disturbing trend of students "breathing" on paper:

> Global warming is . . . (I took a breath so I better put in a comma) . . . becoming a great danger to . . . (uh oh, another breath, so another comma) . . . the world . . . (breath, comma) . . . and all of . . . (well, I took two breaths here, so two commas it is)

In truth, commas have very little to do with pausing and absolutely nothing to do with breathing. Traditionally, commas are instead used to separate particular words or parts of a sentence—excluding their use in lists, addresses, and so on. Here are a few of the most common uses:

- To separate the two parts of a compound sentence, which is when you take two simple sentences and combine them with a conjunction such as *and* or *but*: *Using commas isn't too difficult,* but *you must practice a great deal to master them.*
- To separate two or more adjectives in a row (words describing nouns, such as *thoughtful, passionate* essay).
- To frame sentence interruptions. An interruption is extra information included in a sentence that isn't absolutely necessary: You can, *through a great deal of practice and the right guidance,* become a better writer.

- To separate introductory words or phrases from the rest of a sentence: *Basically*, I'm talking about a sentence like this one you're reading. *You see*, both of these sentences have a word or phrase in their beginnings that are set off from the remaining words.

Run-on and Fused Sentences

Many students obsess about the lengths of their sentences, perhaps due to past composition teachers scaring them to death about run-ons. Many learners feel as if they're committing some sacrilege if they place more than one *and* in a single sentence.

In all honesty, there are no hard-and-fast rules about how many *ands* can exist in a sentence or even what really constitutes a run-on, as there are occasions when a very long sentence is appropriate. Just look at a few works by professional writers, including this book, and you're sure to find such sentences. Still, we do indeed want to avoid crafting statements that are too long and complicated, as this can confuse and frustrate our readers.

Here's an example of a typical run-on sentence:

> General Custer is well known for his failed attack on a Sioux village near Little Bighorn and the massacre that followed, and certainly this was an important event in his life and in the so-called Indian Wars themselves, but there are many other interesting aspects of General Custer that aren't well known, especially his marriages to several Native American women and his heroics in the Civil War, and these certainly deserve some attention, as they were quite significant in the development of his character and his ego, which . . .

Rather than simply worry about the length—though a sentence this long should raise some red flags—it's best to consider how many different ideas are being expressed all at once. Like paragraphs, sentences should be cohesive, meaning that we should avoid trying to stuff too many ideas into a single statement.

This isn't to say all sentences should be short, as such a lack of variety would create incredibly boring prose, but rather that each should state and develop one idea: "development" meaning additional details (though not too many), a clarification of meaning, an example, and so forth. Realize, however, that this is a suggestion, not a rule. Remember what we said about rules?

Sticking with this idea, let's look at that earlier example again. This time, the really long sentences have been split into shorter, more cohesive ones:

> General Custer is well known for his failed attack on a Sioux village near Little Bighorn and the massacre that followed. Certainly this was an important event in his life and in the so-called Indian Wars themselves, but there are many other interesting aspects of General Custer that aren't well known. This is especially true of his marriages to several Native American women and his heroics in the Civil War. These certainly deserve some attention, as they were quite significant in the development of his character and his ego.

As you can see, there were only a few changes made to the original, and yet the revised version now displays better punctuation and better sentence variety and rhythm, and likely is far more pleasurable for weary eyes to read.

The solution is fairly simple: avoid cramming too many thoughts into a single sentence. If you have this tendency, it's perfectly fine to write your rough draft as you normally would, run-ons and all, but make sure you go back through the text and revise such confusing passages. Your readers, including your instructors, will thank you.

MONICA'S PROGRESS

Throughout the semester, Monica worked on her mechanical abilities, especially the problems she was having with fragments, commas, and run-on sentences. She did, however, cut herself a bit of slack after realizing that developing a mastery of these skills takes a great deal of time and practice—time spent pushing through actual, sustained writing.

So, instead of worrying endlessly about grammar and punctuation errors, she focused on all the other aspects of effective writing. You should do the same, especially as you confront them in the following chapters. Always remember that mechanics are in reality a very small part of the writing process. Indeed, there are many other significant aspects upon which to focus.

DISCUSSION QUESTIONS

1. What mechanical aspects of writing do you find especially difficult (commas, possessives, semicolons, verb-tense agreement, and so forth)? What opportunities for practice exist in your daily life?
2. Besides the mechanical issues explained in this chapter, what three elements of punctuation and/or grammar seem most important to you in the production of good writing? Why are these so important?
3. Describe "good writing" or what makes an essay "good" without referring to any mechanical elements (this includes punctuation, grammar, spelling, and vocabulary). Also, explain why these nonmechanical aspects are so critical in creating so-called good writing.

IN-CLASS EXERCISE

This exercise is intended to help you recognize the true role of mechanics in writing. Write a one-page essay in which you describe your favorite music or musical groups. Here's the challenge: You must write this entire page without using any punctuation or following any grammatical rules. That's right—no periods, commas, question marks, capitalization, and so on. You may even spell words as you see fit.

After you've finished, form a small group with two to three fellow students and attempt to read one another's essays out loud.

AT-HOME ASSIGNMENT

Use the Internet to research works by several modern fiction authors, paying close attention to their obedience to or dismissal of conventional mechanical rules.

After doing this, compare and contrast these qualities with those you see in your other textbooks or nonfiction articles. Finally, write a half-page response to the following question: Why do so many successful fiction authors seem to ignore mechanical rules, while nonfiction writers appear far more rigid in their adherence to them? Might it have something to do with their audience's expectations? Explain.

Thinking about such issues can help you understand and develop your own personal writing style.

Chapter Two

Development: Writing Beyond the Facts

JAMES'S STORY

James is a college junior, and he's been putting off the required composition class for more than two years. After finally enrolling and spending the initial several weeks of class attending as infrequently as possible, he is at last forced to submit his first writing assignment: a four- to five-page informational essay about a topic of his choice.

Ever the procrastinator, James finally starts the paper a day before it is due. But that, of course, is no problem—like so many others, he believes he writes better under pressure anyway. And there's nothing like staring at a blank computer screen at 1 a.m. the morning before an assignment is due to generate mounds of pressure, right?

After two hours, James manages to get several paragraphs on the screen, puffing up the paper with lots of long quotes and even a colorful chart. Still, he is only able to reach the middle of page 3, officially giving him two-and-a-half pages of text.

Exhausted and certain the four-page minimum is simply a suggestion, James prints out his paper and goes to bed, confident that his hard (and rather brief) work will earn a good grade.

Unfortunately, he's likely wrong. All too often, students like James misunderstand the reasons behind a word or page requirement, mistakenly believing it is unimportant or designed to frustrate or overwhelm learners.

Actually, word and page minimums are intended to ensure students provide appropriate levels of detail and development in their essays. While it is indeed possible to write a great paper that falls short of these minimums, this is a rare occurrence—quite rare. Nine times out of ten, a short paper lacks adequate development.

Almost always, an instructor interprets this failure as a simple message:

> *Dear Professor,*
> *I just don't care.*
> *Sincerely,*
> *Your Student*

WHAT IS DEVELOPMENT, AND WHY DOES IT MATTER?

Basically, "developing" your ideas and paragraphs is a matter of offering specific details, examples, and explanations that help your readers better understand the material. Doing so makes your writing clearer, more vivid, and ultimately more useful to your audience. Often, a text is developed through one or more of the following methods:

- Providing substantial and relevant detail
- Fully investigating and/or explaining a concept's complexities
- Critically examining an issue's implications, effects, context, and/or the voices conversing about it
- Exploring possible connections to other, often larger, ideas

This is a tall order, to be sure, but it is at the heart of good writing, regardless of the genre. To illustrate the importance of practicing and accomplishing all of this, we will, for a moment, move away from academic writing to an area with which you may be more familiar.

Let's say you receive an email from your best friend that reads as follows: "Last night didn't go well. I got arrested and am out on bail." At that moment, your imagination would undoubtedly run wild, perhaps as it is right now. After receiving the email, what would be your next move? Would you simply return to whatever it was you were doing without giving the message another thought?

Doubtful. It's more likely that you would instead call your friend and find out the details. Without such elaboration, you'd be left in the dark, unable (one would hope) to understand why your best friend was arrested and what might happen as a result.

Developed writing is, of course, important to more than the odd email; your future careers will almost surely require some written communication skills, and detailed explanations are vital in most industries.

It's understandable that few students have any intention of studying or really even regularly using writing beyond their classes. Most look forward to rewarding careers in business, engineering, medicine, technology, industry, or law enforcement. As such, they are often under the mistaken impression that detailed writing will play little to no role in their futures.

Writing instructors have heard just about every justification for this viewpoint that exists. "Businesses value writing that's to the point," one might say. Another may insist that "as long as I'm good with this or that machine, then they won't care about my writing." Wrong. Frighteningly wrong. Being able to adequately explore and explain an idea will prove important in your intended careers. Don't believe it?

- Working in business, your supervisor asks you to write a report investigating and explaining methods to better market a product, reach a group of clients, fix a reoccurring accounting error, or justify the growing expenditures of your department. Don't you think your boss will want some details, a piece of writing that really explores the complexities of the issue?

- Working as a police officer, you make an important arrest and must write a report. You soon realize that the suspect's lawyers will dissect every sentence, looking for anything that might damage your credibility and/or convince a jury to exonerate their client. Do you believe a superficial paragraph will do?

- Working in the tech industry, you're asked to create a manual about the company's latest software, one that customers who are barely computer literate can understand. "Make sure it's impressive and at least twenty pages," your boss says. "That won't be a problem. Right?"

Your writing instructors know that this is a reality in most industries, especially in the modern world, where most positions require significant multitasking. Word and page requirements are their way of pushing you to practice the sustained writing that you will one day, in all likelihood, confront in your careers.

Remember, writing is improved through such practice, not through the rote memorization of grammar and punctuation rules, so to get better and prepare for these futures, you simply must get comfortable with sustained, detailed, critical writing.

THE BIG QUESTION: HOW?

Now that you know you should develop your papers and meet minimum word and page requirements, most of you are almost certainly wondering how to go about accomplishing this seemingly impossible feat. To start, look at a paragraph from James's latest essay:

> Steroid use in professional sports has reached epidemic levels. There have been so many athletes accused of steroid abuse in recent years that many people are calling for harsher punishments for those discovered "juicing up." If this issue isn't resolved soon, professional sports will continue to suffer problems.

It's a tidy paragraph, which is a nice way of saying it is too brief and vague. Even more significant, the paragraph really doesn't tell readers anything beyond common knowledge. Most people are aware that steroid abuse in professional sports has recently garnered a good deal of media attention, so if James hoped to inform his audience, he's fallen short of that goal by telling readers what they already know.

There are several methods we can use to develop this paragraph further, and we can begin with the first of those aforementioned pillars of strong writing: *providing substantial and relevant detail.* Look at the parts of James's paragraph that are vague—we aren't given any specifics about the athletes being accused, the nature of the "harsher punishments" being proposed, or even what "problems" professional sports will suffer if the issue isn't addressed.

All of these are perfect opportunities for providing additional, specific detail. For our purposes, we'll add more detail to the latter two sentences:

Steroid use in professional sports has reached epidemic levels. There have been so many athletes accused of steroid abuse in recent years that many people are calling for harsher punishments for those discovered "juicing up." *For example, some critics have suggested that athletes convicted of steroid abuse should be banned from their sports of choice, while others have demanded the retraction of such an athlete's trophies and records.* If this issue isn't resolved soon, professional sports will continue to suffer problems, *including a dramatic loss of credibility in the eyes of fans and the world.*

With a few additions, including some specific examples, we've already improved this paragraph a great deal. There are, of course, several other ways you might have added more detail; in writing, there is rarely a single right answer—writers leave that to mathematicians. The more you practice being specific, however, the better you will become at determining (by intuition alone) how much more detail a paragraph needs and where it should appear.

Obviously, your essay will consist of more than one paragraph—at least it should. As such, simply adding additional details will be insufficient in giving your assignment the development it needs. Generating ideas for other paragraphs also proves difficult for many students. "I don't know what else to write!" they often say, as if prepared to beat themselves with their keyboards.

In James's case, he tried to make up for a lack of direction and ideas by repeating the same concepts again and again, simply phrasing each instance differently. To focus his efforts at paragraph and idea generation, he should instead contemplate the second development option: *fully investigate and explain the topic's complexities.*

As with any topic worth writing about, there are plenty of complexities James could explore. For instance, he might examine various sides of the current debate, the relationship between steroids and legal supplements, or the difficulties in detecting abuse and enforcing rules in professional sports. On a deeper level, he could also investigate what the issue says about the values of American society—is it possibly society's fault that athletes are willing to jeopardize their lives to gain an edge on the competition? Ultimately, there are plenty of options open to the aware and willing writer. It's simply a matter of discovering and pursuing them.

After spending a few hours wallowing in self-pity about his lack of ideas, James at last decides to explore the difficulties with detecting steroid abuse and enforcing the rules against it. With a good deal of work—and an eye on providing sufficient detail—he manages to write the following. For clarity, the introduction has been included as well:

> Steroid use in professional sports has reached epidemic levels. There have been so many athletes accused of steroid abuse in recent years that many people are calling for harsher punishments for those discovered "juicing up." For example, some critics have suggested that athletes convicted of steroid abuse should be banned from their sport of choice, while others have demanded the retraction of such an athlete's trophies and records. If this issue isn't resolved soon, professional sports will continue to suffer problems, including a dramatic loss of credibility in the eyes of fans and the world.
>
> Of course, calling for a resolution to an athlete's problem and overcoming the difficulties associated with it are quite different, especially regarding steroid detection and enforcement. With their careers in jeopardy, many professional athletes have become experts at concealing their use of steroids. According to Dr. Marcus Knight, an expert in drug testing, "Any and all tests have flaws. Chronic steroid abusers can and have found numerous ways to pass them on a regular basis" (203). Dr. Knight also suggests that testing alone cannot dissuade chemical abuse; it must work in tandem with real and immediate consequences placed upon athletes by their respective leagues.
>
> Ideas about what those consequences should look like and when they should be applied vary among experts, fans, and sports officials. The Hoover Institute for Sports Science recently conducted a poll that concluded that 78 percent of fans believe

athletes convicted of steroid abuse should be banned from their respective sports, while only 25 percent of coaches and team owners agreed with such a course of action (87–88). Put simply, these polls suggest that sports officials may lack the strict attitude necessary to combat drug abuse within their leagues. Fans, on the other hand, are apparently growing tired of being disappointed by their sports heroes and heroines, and they are demanding change.

These are pretty decent paragraphs—not perfect by any stretch of the imagination—but they at least display a sense of structure, specific and relevant details, and purpose. If necessary, James can decide to explore similar ideas, or he might investigate the third aspect of well-developed writing mentioned earlier—namely, *the probable implications and/or effects this issue may generate*. If he is writing a persuasive essay, in which he hopes to convince an audience of a stance rather than simply educate readers, he should also respond to challenges from opponents.

As this paper is purely informational, James decides to examine what might happen should sports leagues fail to address the problem. Remember, this new paragraph would normally immediately follow the passages above:

The perceptions of those fans, in addition to the obviously important moral aspects of the issue, should be enough to spur change in how professional sports leagues approach steroid abuse. After all, such leagues depend entirely on the support of fans for their very existence. One can certainly imagine the potential financial disaster if fans suddenly stopped buying tickets for events or purchasing the associated merchandise. Last year alone, ticket sales for professional sports topped $300 million (Winchester 156). If even half of sports fans stopped attending events, league after league would surely find itself in turmoil. The immense salaries that many athletes enjoy would dry up, and teams would see merchandising revenue vanish.

Obviously, James's essay is really coming along. While he is still far short of the word and page requirements, he has some momentum behind his writing and is beginning to understand what development really means.

To flesh out the rest of the essay, he should continue exploring other specific aspects of the issue, each in a single, well-detailed paragraph. He could, for example, investigate the reasons steroids are banned in professional sports, provide real-world stories of athletes who have suffered from the effects of such drugs, analyze recent studies on the health effects of steroid abuse, examine other possible consequences should the problem be ignored, and so on.

Remember, the three *E*'s are what matter most in development: *E*xamine the issue's specifics. *E*xplore its complexities and possible consequences. *E*xplain it all in a clear manner that readers will take seriously.

As James nears his essay's conclusion, he should also seek to *investigate any connections that may exist between his topic and larger ideas*: reflections on society, the human condition, the world, and so forth. For instance, as asked earlier in the chapter, is the steroid abuse issue a symptom of some larger and deeper problem in professional sports and American society itself? If so, exploring and explaining that connection would be a powerful addition to the essay. Likewise, does such abuse say something about our shared human experience, especially our sense of competitiveness? If yes, we'd definitely want to touch on that.

Recognizing these connections can often prove difficult, and if you find yourself stuck, ask yourself the following questions: Why does the issue matter, and why should readers care?

For a moment, imagine that James's readers are anything but sports fans. They've never attended a game, don't watch sports on television, and really just don't care about who wins and who loses.

Why should such readers care about steroid abuse in professional sports? And don't give in to lazy thinking here, as we can definitely think of a few reasons:

- James might contend that the number of young fans alone makes the issue important, as those children and teenagers are greatly influenced by their sports heroes and heroines.
- He could explain that professional athletes are representatives of America, both to our own citizens and abroad. Steroid abuse damages our national reputation.
- James may decide to examine how such abuse, like academic cheating, destroys the nature of real accomplishment, turning human achievement into a farce.

Grappling with these larger ideas, with that "so what?" question, is imperative, and it's really where that all-important "critical thinking" is usually found. It also shows your teacher or professor that you are aware of your audience and are writing for your readers rather than simply for yourself.

JAMES'S PROGRESS

Remember that these strategies for developing your essays are just that—strategies, not rules, and certainly not templates. Part of becoming and indeed being a writer is making sometimes difficult decisions, and these include decisions about development.

While James struggled with his paper, at times sentence by sentence, he finally did meet the assignment's required word and page requirements with meaningful writing. Although this does make it more likely that he'll receive a decent grade, the real importance rests on the fact that his essay is now more developed, specific, and useful for readers.

Of course, this achievement also made the paper more useful for James himself, as it has forced him to expand and deepen his thinking, to consider possibilities and ideas he might have otherwise ignored, and to improve his abilities at explaining complicated concepts. This will not only prove useful in his future classes and even his eventual career but also help him participate more effectively in the important social discussions affecting his community.

DISCUSSION QUESTIONS

1. Think carefully about your future plans and potential career. How will writing play a role in that career? What specific writing tasks will you likely be required to complete, and what rhetorical skills will prove most important and useful in that field?
2. Imagine a fellow student is having difficulty understanding the development concepts and techniques discussed in this chapter. How would you explain the purposes of minimum page or word requirements and why they are necessary? In other words, why must a writer fully develop his or her essay?

IN-CLASS EXERCISE OR AT-HOME ASSIGNMENT

On the next page, you will see three sentences. Each represents the topic sentence for a paragraph that needs further development—more details, examples, evidence, and so forth. Unfortunately, the original author is uncertain of how to do this. Assist the author by developing each paragraph, using the techniques discussed in this chapter for guidance.

1. While often expensive and difficult, earning a college degree provides numerous benefits.
2. Selecting a college or university can also prove difficult, but fully exploring an institution's academic programs can help.
3. Finally, students should also consider the extracurricular opportunities at institutions they're considering.

Chapter Three

Internet Research: There's More to It Than Search Engines

MAYA'S STORY

Unlike Monica and James, Maya didn't start out the semester terrified of writing. As she begins her senior year high school English class, she feels confident in the training she's received thus far concerning mechanics, structure, and development.

Maya's confidence, however, wanes a bit upon seeing a "research paper" listed on the syllabus, as she has very little experience locating sources, using the library's databases, or incorporating what she eventually finds into an essay. In fact, whenever her other teachers required the use of facts or quotes in a paper, Maya "forgot" to include them; yet, somehow, she still earned decent grades.

But her new teacher, she soon discovers, demands that Maya use several "reliable and properly cited sources" to support her essay's claims—and he means it. Unnerved but anxious about her grade, she goes home, jumps on the computer, and types a few keywords into her favorite search engine.

31

Unfortunately, the search engine returns over twenty million matching websites. On her second attempt, after applying some quotation marks to the keywords, she manages to reduce those results to a mere ten million—that's right, ten million—options . . . ten million possible sources through which to scrounge.

Of course, Maya has no intention of examining millions of websites, so she restricts herself to the first few pages of results. Surely these are the best sources anyway, right? Easily enough, she finds a blog and an official-looking article from an online magazine she's never heard of. After scanning each, Maya locates an interesting quote and a set of statistics, plunks them into her essay, and calls it a night. Quotes found. Statistics copied and pasted. Research done.

Sadly, this is how most students approach research, and, like Maya, most will be rewarded with low grades on their essays.

THE WEB AND RESEARCH

Let's start by calming your fears and alleviating your doubts: the Internet is indeed a wonderful tool for research . . . if used properly. Up until the widespread use of the Web, researching an issue normally involved long hours at a library, stacks of books and periodicals, and a willingness to scrounge through texts in pursuit of directly relevant information. For many of you, this probably sounds like a nightmare, especially when you can now simply log on to the Web, use a search engine, and instantly have an almost endless array of sources sprawled out before you.

While the Internet has absolutely changed the way most students conduct research, it hasn't necessarily made all aspects of the process easier or better. For example, when a person was forced to scour physical library shelves, he or she could be far more confident in the reliability of those books and periodicals. This isn't to say that all the information contained in printed sources is accurate, but rather that the costs and difficulties of printing actual books, journals, and magazines usually drive higher editorial standards and fact checking.

Think about it this way: If you were a book publisher spending hundreds of thousands of dollars on the printing of a single text, you would likely go to great lengths to ensure the information contained therein was accurate. To that end, you would surely verify an author's credentials, have trained editors carefully examine each and every sentence of the text, and complete a series of revisions until the book was as perfect as possible. After all, if the final printed text contains serious flaws, your company will either have to print an expensive correction or risk plugging huge amounts of money into an unreliable flop.

The same isn't true of the Web. The cost of registering a domain name and creating a website are incredibly inexpensive when compared to producing and printing a physical book or magazine. Because of this, nearly anyone with a few bucks to burn and an opinion can set up a site and pass himself or herself off as an expert. And with the array of software available these days, most can make a website look sophisticated and entirely professional. In short, Bob in Alabama can easily pretend to be a German astrophysicist, while Brenda in California can disguise herself as one of China's top medical doctors. Even whole organizations can ignore basic editing standards and fact checking; after all, if an error is discovered on the website, making a change is quite simple and cheap.

As implied earlier, there are indeed many reputable and reliable sites and sources on the Web, but all too often they are absolutely drowning in a sea of the deceptive, the ignorant, the overly biased, and the utterly ridiculous. If you choose to focus your research efforts online, part of your job will be to recognize the good sources among all the other not-so-good ones.

RESEARCH AND EVIDENCE . . . WHAT'S THE POINT?

In class, students are often told to "use quotes and evidence to support what you want to say, not replace it." Most probably get tired of hearing this statement, but the meaning is important: the products of research (e.g., quotes, facts, statistics, examples, etc.) should be used to support and/or illustrate your writing, not provide the writing itself.

When conducting research, therefore, we strive to accomplish two primary goals: First, we want to develop a strong understanding of the topic, its context, its voices, and its complexities. Second, we conduct research to help us explain and prove our claims and conclusions to an audience. Many students are fairly good at the second goal, but few realize the learning opportunities found in research—learning that is often at the heart of an assignment's purpose.

Every writer (novice and veteran alike) should approach an assignment with this truism in mind. Yes, research is a chance to locate studies or like-minded experts who will help us support our opinions and conclusions, but we should first and foremost depend on it as a way to educate ourselves about a topic and critically examine our beliefs about it.

Undoubtedly, there are students out there who hear this mantra about using evidence to support rather than replace one's writing and don't know how to write about a given topic without depending entirely on quotes they find online. "How?" they ask, dumbfounded. "Shouldn't I just tell readers what the experts say about it? How can I educate an audience about this or that topic when I don't know much about it?"

Quite simply, you can't.

If you know nothing about a topic beyond common knowledge, beyond what your readers already know, there's little point in writing an essay about it. Imagine for a moment that one of your professors, regardless of subject, knew nothing more than you did about the topics being discussed in class. Would you really benefit from that course? Would you grow as an intellectual? If you're paying tuition, would you be angry?

Therefore, you must conduct research to develop an expertise about the topic you choose. This isn't to say that you must become an environmental scientist to write about climate change or a lawyer to examine problems in the judicial system; it simply means that you must explore a topic, learn about it, move past common knowledge, and provide your readers with something of value.

Once you have developed this understanding, you can then educate an audience all by yourself, only using the experts to support and illustrate your points.

METHODS FOR CHOOSING SOURCES

Obviously, choosing a source simply based upon its placement in a search engine's results is a poor method. After all, in addition to a site's particular keywords, its placement on a typical search engine's results page often depends on (1) the website's popularity, (2) a site owner's willingness to pay for priority placement, or (3) the sheer amount of content on a particular site. None of these qualities add to a source's credibility, especially in the eyes of a skeptical academic audience—for example, your teachers and professors.

While there is some disagreement among writing instructors about what constitutes a reliable source, most seem to agree on the following characteristics:

1. *True Expertise:* The source's author (either a person or organization) has the credentials to back up the claims being made. For example, if you were feeling ill, whose opinion would you trust more: that of a medical doctor at your local hospital or one from a random stranger you met on the street?
2. *Publication Date:* The source's publication date suggests it is up to date on modern discoveries, debates, and/or information about the topic. This is especially important for papers concerning science, technology, and politics, as topics within these categories are constantly changing. For instance, would an article about computers from 1965 really be up to date?
3. *Obvious Bias:* While every source contains some bias, as does every human being, some authors and organizations allow their biases to interfere with the accuracy of their claims (sometimes knowingly). Take care when using sources that have something to gain from the results of a given study, and be especially skeptical of a study paid for by that author or organization.
4. *URL:* Usually, academic audiences more readily embrace information from websites ending in with .edu (education), .mil (military), or .gov (government) in the Uniform Resource Locator (URL) address. While there is no guarantee that such sites contain accurate information, the fact that they cannot usually be purchased by the general public normally makes them more reliable than .com (commercial), .org (organization), or .net (network).

There are, of course, other qualities often associated with a source's credibility, but underlying them all is this truism: like beauty, credibility "is in the eyes of the beholder." In other words, the "rules" listed here and in most other composition textbooks don't really determine a source's reliability—your audience does.

When conducting research and choosing sources, think about your readers: What will they consider a good source? Whom will they probably believe? In short, what source will most help you accomplish your goal of educating and/or convincing an audience?

Advertising agencies already know that name recognition sells, which is why they hire celebrities to endorse their products rather than true experts. For instance, how often do you see a podiatrist (a doctor specializing in feet) on a sneaker commercial? I'd wager you see a basketball or football star far more often. The same is true of weight-loss programs. Rather than get a real specialist who may just spout a bunch of scientific mumbo jumbo, it's best to hire a slim actor or actress who will simply read the provided script. Such instances are certainly no accident, and they are normally quite effective with general audiences.

Your audience, of course, is far more skeptical, and you should assume your readers will find celebrity endorsements less than impressive.

Below, you'll find several examples that should help solidify this in your mind. For each, think about how your instructor or professor would likely react if it appeared in a paper—and yes, the names are completely fictional:

1. According to David Coolridge, a star wide receiver at Victory Lane University, climate change is real and the biggest threat to humanity's future.
2. Deborah James, a spokesperson for several fast food companies, states that eating cheeseburgers every day can actually be a healthy lifestyle choice. Therefore, we should encourage this kind of diet in our schools.
3. My mother's best friend works in law enforcement, and he told her that more needs to be done in schools about preserving art and music programs.

Don't laugh. Students use similar sources to support claims all the time. They're presented here not to poke fun but rather to show you what ineffective sources look like. Let's now compare them to much stronger sources, using the same topics mentioned above. How would your instructor or professor react?

1. According to Dr. Barbara Daunting, an environmental scientist at Victory Lane University, climate change is real and the biggest threat to humanity's future.
2. Certified nutritionist Peter Xiong states that eating cheeseburgers every day can have a tremendously negative impact on a person's overall health.
3. Lisa Garcia, a public school superintendent, suggests that more needs to be done in schools about preserving art and music programs.

It's pretty obvious that the second set of sources is far superior, if only because they all possess verifiable expertise in the subjects being examined. Remember, paying attention to a source's credentials isn't effective because it's a "rule"; it's a rule because it's usually effective.

THE SOURCES YOU'RE LIKELY NEGLECTING

Many high schools and most colleges and universities these days offer students a way to take advantage of the Web's convenience while simultaneously avoiding unreliable sources: online library databases. Even better, schools almost always make access to these enormous online collections free to their students.

Rather than endlessly searching the Web for the right article or book—usually only to find that the full text is either unavailable or pricey—a student can access the database from home and easily find treasure troves of hand-selected, full-text materials on nearly every subject imaginable.

This brings up another important point, one that may seem elementary, but still bears explaining: If your school has a library (especially a multimillion-dollar one, which is quite common), you should absolutely visit it in person whenever you're researching a topic. Most institutions go to extraordinary lengths to ensure that their libraries are brimming with articles, journals, newspapers, encyclopedias, textbooks, novels, biographies, and nonfiction books. Yet some students never even set foot inside the campus library. In fact, many seem confused by it, even terrified. Realize, however, that those resources can be very helpful, and the library itself often offers a peaceful study environment that is rarely found elsewhere.

It's also recommended that you get to know a few of the librarians. Many students are under the mistaken impression that all librarians do is check out and reshelve books, which is completely ridiculous. Librarians are highly educated experts in research, and their familiarity with the collections can be invaluable, especially if you find yourself stuck.

MAYA'S PROGRESS

Although she endured a few intellectual bumps and bruises, Maya did at last develop a stronger understanding of research, its role in academic writing, and techniques for locating reliable sources. More importantly, her capacity to look beyond the superficial requirements of a writing assignment and see the underlying learning opportunities grew as well.

No longer were assignments simply about generating text, informing an audience, building an argument, or even earning a good grade. Instead, Maya began to recognize and embrace the true, though often forgotten, promise of higher education: the ability to think critically for oneself and participate effectively in society.

DISCUSSION QUESTIONS

1. Imagine you're writing an essay on the challenges of educating special needs children in elementary schools. How would you conduct your research and differentiate effective sources from ineffective ones? How might your growing understanding of academic audiences affect your decisions?
2. Explore the research resources your school, college, or university offers: What resources are available, how does one access them, and how can you use what's available while writing your next essay?

IN-CLASS EXERCISE

Imagine your next writing assignment is a twenty-page research paper on the origins of the video game industry. When confronted with an assignment of this size and complexity, it's often helpful to create a research schedule for yourself, as doing so keeps the information-gathering process organized and productive.

A blank, two-week schedule form has been provided for your convenience. Work with your peers in a small group, and complete the form with specific tasks, benchmarks, and goals. Try to avoid vague entries like "conduct research" or "search the Internet," and include items that refer to specific sources, source types, or methods. Also, feel free to include a little time off—but not *too* much. Remember, such a schedule can only be as helpful as you make it.

Day	Research Task or Goal (Week 1)
1	
2	
3	
4	
5	
6	
7	

Day	Research Task or Goal (Week 2)
1	
2	
3	
4	
5	
6	
7	

AT-HOME ASSIGNMENT

For each of the following topics, use the Internet or your school's digital databases to locate two credible academic sources. For each source you find, provide an author and title, and also include a short summary (two to three sentences) of its content.

- The Battle of Iwo Jima during World War II
- The Future of Space Exploration
- Scarcity of Healthy Food Options in Urban Centers

Chapter Four

Computers and Composition

BRANDI'S STORY

Besides her family and her boyfriend, Brandi has one great love in her life: technology. For instance, while only a sophomore in high school, she has become a grand master in the art of texting during class and is able to conceal her keystrokes and conversations from even the sharpest-eyed instructor.

Her skills with a computer and the Internet are equally impressive. Brandi can surf a dozen websites, post updates on her favorite social networking sites, and study her favorite band's upcoming tour dates with amazing speed.

What about academic research, you ask? No problem! When her English teacher assigns a paper, Brandi simply jumps online, moving quickly and efficiently from site to site, and gathers more information than she could ever possibly use. Of course, when it is actually time to use all that research—the facts, the figures, the quotes from reliable websites, and so forth—she finds herself somewhat less effective.

"Paralyzed" might be a more accurate description.

ADRIFT UPON AN OCEAN OF RESEARCH

As we saw in the last chapter, the Internet is an incredibly powerful research tool, allowing anyone with a connection to access a sea of information. Obviously, choosing reliable and appropriate sources from that seemingly infinite expanse can be difficult and danger- ous, but locating good information is only part of the battle. Even- tually, we must decide what to include in our papers and then actually do it. While this may sound easy, many novice writers have no idea how to go about it.

Here's the thing: Many of you out there grew up with the Inter- net and are accustomed to using search engines and having imme- diate access to whatever information you wanted. Want to know your favorite singer's birthday and biography? With a few clicks of your mouse, you've got it. Want to explore the history of your town, common psychological disorders, the moon landing, the Spanish translation for "I need to visit the restroom, please," or any other intellectual curiosity that strikes you? Done!

In truth, most of you are already decent online researchers. Like Brandi, you're likely quite good at finding information on the Web—perhaps too good. Often, a new writing assignment sends students scurrying to their computers, and within an hour many are absolutely drowning in information. As the bookmarked websites, saved files, and printed pages begin to stack up, their desperation grows. As their desperation grows, the more research they feel compelled to conduct.

This cycle can and often does derail even the most enthusiastic students and best writers. Uncertain about what to do with all the information they've collected but unwilling to surrender any of the data they've worked so hard to get, some try to stuff it all into a few pages of writing. Others, mired in the research process, only get around to the actual essay itself at the last minute. As you might suspect, that doesn't normally turn out well.

Like many other aspects of good writing, deciding which information to include and how to incorporate it is often a balancing act: you want to include enough to support your points but not so much that it overwhelms your readers and buries your points.

CHOICES, CHOICES . . .

So how does one go about deciding what to include? As you may already suspect, there isn't an absolute rule governing such choices. Instead, you must develop your instincts through continued practice while keeping the following guidelines in mind:

- *Evidence that possesses some emotional component impacts many readers more profoundly than purely logical data.* Think about it: Which of the following would move you more—a statistic showing how many people die of lung cancer every year or a short description of one woman's battle with the disease?
- *Try to use different sorts of evidence to support your points rather than the same kind over and over again.* Human beings tend to enjoy and respond to variety. Can you imagine eating the same meal, day after day, week after week? In one paragraph, use a statistic and a quote; in the next, use an example and a fact, and so on. Your readers will likely appreciate the shifting combinations.
- *If you have five sources that say the same thing, use only one or two, preferably the strongest and most reputable of the group.* Sometimes, you may need to use several sources when supporting a complex or controversial point, but it's often best to avoid such redundancy. One or two well-worded and well-incorporated pieces of evidence can prove more effective than a throng of others.

Remember, these are only guidelines, not rules. Consider your topic, the nature of your points and claims, and the expectations of your audience when making a decision. What will probably work best? Will someone likely challenge the evidence you present? Which evidence will help readers understand and trust you?

THE DIRECT APPROACH

Besides saddling students with overbearing amounts of information, modern technology also seems to be having an effect on our collective approach to written communication—specifically, it encourages a direct, to-the-point style that may appear abrupt, choppy, and even downright rude to academic readers.

This is hardly surprising when one considers how efficient we must be when texting one another, when discussing a topic in a chat room, or when posting an update on a social media site. In-depth and/or poetic explanations don't work well in any of these mediums. Would you read an update that went on for a full page?

As such, many of you accustomed to texting or communicating with your friends across cyberspace probably find academic writing drawn out, long-winded, and exhausting. "Can't I just get to the point?" you might shout when reading over your teacher's latest comments, all of which seem to suggest your explanations are too brief.

As suggested in our chapter about development, however, "the point" isn't necessarily the most important aspect of your essay. Remember, you're not simply sending out waves of information at readers; you're exploring and examining and communicating. Equally important to the points in your essay is the rationale behind those conclusions—the ideas and thoughts and reasoning that led you to the point you're making.

An academic audience will want to see this. Academic readers—especially those in the humanities—will want to see details about your topic, the support holding up your assertions, and the justifications for your claims. And they'll want it all packaged in a sophisticated, formal, and aesthetically pleasing writing style. Hurried and "to-the-point" writing simply won't accomplish all this.

In addition, there's yet another reason why instructors dislike abrupt writing: it focuses solely on the end product and conceals a writer's process and reasoning. Do you remember in math class when the teacher insisted you "show your work" when completing a problem? Often, showing the teacher what led you to the answer would reveal whether or not you truly understood the material, especially if you happened to make a mistake along the way.

While there are seldom "right" or "wrong" answers in writing, some conclusions are better reasoned and thus more logically sound than others. By examining your rationale, your teacher or instructor can help you become a better critical thinker, which in turn makes you a better writer.

Ultimately, academic writing isn't really "drawn out" or unnecessarily long-winded. It's simply more thorough and more carefully constructed.

DEALING WITH DISTRACTION

Modern life is distracting. There's simply no denying that the era in which we live is a noisy one, and technology has brought that noise into our homes in unparalleled ways.

It's natural to wonder sometimes what it must have been like to compose in ages past—say, in feudal Japan or Victorian England. If you leave aside little nuisances like plagues, famines, and regular bouts of horrific warfare, surely these eras possessed a peace and quiet absolutely foreign to us.

Our modern world, however, is full of distractions—television, video games, music, and so on. Today, the availability of such distractions has increased tenfold, especially with the widespread use of the Internet. How can the planning or writing of an essay possibly compete? Procrastination, it seems, may be inevitable.

Ultimately, the most effective tool for combating distraction and the procrastination it causes is self-discipline, which no book or teacher can simply give you. The determination to sit down and write the best paper you can write—regardless of what's on television or the newest text message on your phone—rests with you alone.

There are, however, techniques that can help you overcome the "until tomorrow" temptation. One widely used technique is the daily word count. Assigning oneself a word minimum for the day (say, three hundred to five hundred words) is an excellent method to combat distraction and procrastination. This is very common among professional writers—most of whom are also human, by the way.

For example, let's say an English instructor assigns you a research paper of eight to ten pages, which amounts to two thousand to three thousand words, and she says the rough draft is due in a month's time. Undoubtedly, many of you would find this intimidating; some may even find it absolutely terrifying. Fortunately, you have four whole weeks to finish it, which means you can break up this larger paper into more manageable pieces.

Obviously, there are a few ways to do this: You could choose to write only one hundred words a day, or perhaps you're more ambitious and think five hundred is reasonable. In any case, you assign yourself a daily *chunk* of writing and focus on that piece rather than the whole paper. This makes the task less intimidating, and it often enables novice and professional writers alike to produce better work.

Ultimately, this simple method will help you establish a pattern of disciplined writing, a habit that can eventually develop its own drive and momentum. It's rarely easy, and the desire to watch a television show or check up on friends will often creep into your mind if the words and the keyboard just refuse to cooperate, but don't allow such distractions to rule your thinking and behavior.

BRANDI'S PROGRESS

Brandi still loves her computer and cell phone. Throughout the semester, however, she gained a better understanding of their often-unnoticed effects on her writing habits. While her research capabilities still regularly outperform her skills at incorporating it into an actual paper, practice and a little teacher guidance at least narrowed the gap between them. Steadily, her papers and the grades they receive have improved over the last several months, along with her sense of writing discipline and her approach to the academic audience actually reading her texts.

The latter of these advances is perhaps the most profound, as it indicates a change in her attitude toward writing itself. Specifically, when one views the written word as merely a means of communication, as the moving of information from one brain to another, efficiency is naturally prized above all other qualities. But writing isn't just a method of communication. Instead, it's a means to and an expression of human connection, and it must be treated as such.

DISCUSSION QUESTIONS

1. Briefly consider and then describe your writing habits. How do you approach the writing of an essay? Do you attempt to complete a project in one sitting, or do you break up the work among several sessions? How does technology affect those habits in your own life?

2. Analyze and describe your own online writing style. Does your writing tend to be blunt and to the point, flowery, jumbled, or disjointed? How does this style compare to or contrast with your writing in an academic essay? What changes, if any, should you make to your writing style that will make it more appropriate for an academic audience?

IN-CLASS EXERCISE

Five different topic sentences are listed below—all fairly brief and directly to the point. Develop each into a full paragraph that better reflects a tone and content appropriate for academic writing. Add whatever details you believe are necessary.

1. Technology has changed the world and will continue to do so for years to come.

2. The Internet is a good tool for research, but it can also cause problems.

3. Research is important, but a huge assortment of sources isn't enough to write a good paper.

4. Developing self-discipline is a major part of becoming a stronger writer.

5. Academic readers usually value critical thinking and a willingness to fully explore an issue.

AT-HOME ASSIGNMENT

Carefully examine your favorite websites, social media networks, and even the text messages you exchange with close friends. After doing so, write a brief (one-page) essay in which you respond to the following question: What can these writing styles possibly tell us about our modern world, its general values, and its possible future?

After finishing the essay, consider what your own writing style may say about you as a member of that modern community.

Chapter Five

The Writing Process: Finding a Topic, Drafting, and Fleshing It Out

JAVIER'S STORY

Poor Javier. In previous classes, the teachers always assigned paper topics: "Write a report about the life of Mark Twain"; "Give me two pages summarizing *Romeo and Juliet*"; "Write a paper about what you did during the last summer vacation." Sure, most of those topics were boring, but at least he knew what to write about and could muddle through it, if pressed.

Unfortunately for Javier, his new high school English teacher is far more liberal in her topic assignments and has given each student free rein in selecting one of his or her choosing. "Write a persuasive essay about a topic you think is important," she said, as if she was doing everyone a favor. "Oh, and make sure it's appropriate for scholarly discussion."

It was the second half of the teacher's instructions that really stumped Javier. He could definitely think of an important topic with little trouble, especially as the college basketball season was really heating up. If he could just write about that, he'd have no trouble filling up three or more pages. After all, he already knew all of the necessary statistics.

Of course, writing about college basketball didn't seem to meet the teacher's second demand: "Make sure it's appropriate for scholarly discussion." He hadn't seen any scholars teaching classes on basketball statistics, and there were definitely none discussing his opinions about this team or that.

APPROPRIATE FOR SCHOLARLY DISCUSSION . . .

To start, when a teacher or professor demands that your topic be appropriate for scholarly discussion, what he or she is really requiring is that you choose a topic that scholars from one of the various academic disciplines might discuss (e.g., the humanities, fine arts, life sciences, physical sciences, social sciences, etc.). To be blunt, he or she probably isn't interested in your opinions concerning sports, movies, music, cars, or the opposite sex.

As far as the assignment goes, he or she doesn't care what athletes you admire, what kind of car you'd love to own, what you personally hate about current traffic laws, or that your favorite uncle's former roommate is a movie star. Instead, your teacher or professor is asking you to write about one of the important discussions going on in academia and/or society.

This may seem quite limiting, even intimidating, as perhaps you don't really know or care about any topic in the academic disciplines. Maybe you're uncertain about your interests and have no desire to write about such topics as the need to change how exceptional children are educated or the morality of a society based on pure relativism. These issues have nothing to do with your immediate life, they probably never will, and you'd much rather ask the instructor for permission to write a biography of your uncle's former roommate. Remember? The movie star?

Tough.

As discussed in an earlier chapter, one of the virtues of education is that students are exposed to subjects they would otherwise probably never explore—and in so doing, expand their capacities for deeper thought, for active and effective participation in their communities, and for the benefit of society as a whole.

You want the better job, the higher salary, and the respect that comes with a diploma or degree; however, with those rewards comes responsibility, a responsibility for improving our world, and you can't accomplish that task from within an intellectual shell. Therefore, when you're given an assignment in which you're free to choose an academic or social topic, open yourself up to ideas and issues with which you're unfamiliar. Develop a curiosity about the world, especially about those aspects of it you've never explored.

If you're required to write an informational essay, ask yourself these questions: *What have I always wanted to know more about? Have I read something or seen a show on television that caught my interest? What seems mysterious in the world? What seems really important in people's lives?*

If you're required to write a persuasive or argumentative essay, look at our society and/or our world. What makes you angry? What do you think needs to change, and how should that change occur?

LIMITING FOCUS

Of course, selecting a topic is just half of the task, as there is the danger of it being too broad or too limited. If the topic proves too broad, like one more appropriate for an entire book than a three- to four-page essay, your paper will probably amount to little more than a general overview of an incredibly complex subject. If it ends up being too limited, you'll find yourself with nothing left to write after a single page.

In truth, the former outcome occurs more often than the latter, as many students are so terrified of page requirements that they choose enormous topics—abortion, pollution, gun control, capital punishment, and so on. While there's nothing inherently wrong with these topics—apart from how distressingly often writing instructors must read essays about them—they are far too broad and complicated for anything short of several hundred pages.

Therefore, you should select a smaller aspect of the topic or its surrounding debate upon which to focus. Don't worry. If you research properly and give yourself time, you won't run out of words after only one page. In fact, your essay will be much more effective.

But how does one narrow focus? Let's look at one of those aforementioned popular topics: pollution. Rather than give you a series of confusing charts, we'll walk through the thinking process that should take place in limiting your essay's scope:

1. There are many kinds of pollution, too many to cover. What interests you most? Water pollution? Air pollution? Noise pollution?
2. OK, you select water pollution. This, of course, occurs in different ways and in many different parts of the world. Instead of trying to cover all types of water pollution, perhaps you could focus on a particular type and a particular place: *Industrial Water Pollution* or *Water Pollution in Modern Haiti* or even *Industrial Water Pollution in Modern Haiti.*
3. If you're writing a purely informational paper, you might stop there. If your essay is argumentative, however, you need to go further and consider your stance on the matter. Do things need to change concerning this issue? Perhaps you might try the following: *The Need for International Support in Combating Water Pollution in Haiti.*

Here's another example, broken down in a similar fashion, to help clear up any confusion. In this instance, we'll start with another broad topic—discrimination.

1. As in the previous example, this topic is far too large and complex for the typical school essay. First, we should go ahead and decide what general type of discrimination we want to examine: racial, gender, age, class, sexual orientation, and so forth.

2. We'll select age discrimination for our purposes here—specifically, discrimination against people beyond middle age. Still, despite our quickly narrowing focus, we need to go further.

   In the previous example, we chose to limit ourselves to a particular geography, Haiti, and we could again select a specific geographical location for our essay. Instead, let's select another kind of "place" that might prove more interesting—namely, the workplace: *Ageism in the Workplace* or *Discrimination against Baby Boomers in the Workforce.*

3. Again, if the essay is supposed to be purely informational, you may be able to begin your prewriting without narrowing any further. If you're writing a persuasive piece, however, you must once more incorporate an opinion or argument into the paper. What do you want to say about the topic? More important, what do you want readers to eventually believe about it? Perhaps either of the following would work: *The Absurdity of Ageism in the Workplace* or *The Need for Preventing Discrimination against Baby Boomers in the Workforce.*

Remember, all we're really trying to do is reduce the scope of the essay so we aren't trying to cram the proverbial textual elephant into a shoebox. Realize, however, that this will take practice, and you shouldn't demand perfection of yourself the first few times you attempt it. Be patient with yourself, which, of course, requires giving yourself some time before the paper is due.

Finally, when you at last decide on a focused topic, fight the temptation to simply begin writing the essay. There is some crucial work left to do before taking that leap.

PREWRITING: IT'S MORE THAN BRAINSTORMING

You undoubtedly remember making bubble maps at some point in your education. Remember? The teacher would draw a circle on the board, write a topic inside, and then connect a series of smaller circles to it with random ideas for the content of an essay. Sadly, such bubble maps constitute the entirety of what most students know about prewriting—the stage of writing when one generates ideas before actually writing the paper.

For many of those novice writers, the bubble-map technique never proved very useful, and so they assume that prewriting is a huge waste of time. Of course, such mapping is but one method among many. Freewriting, collaboration, listing, outlining—all of these are options that can and should be explored, as they all help writers think more deeply about their topics, which in turn helps them generate ideas and content.

Often, these methods work best when used in combination with one another, but sometimes you will simply run into a technique that doesn't work for you. If you do, don't force yourself to use it, as that will only frustrate you before even beginning to pen the actual essay.

Freewriting

Most of you have probably tried this technique before. Using this, one simply begins to write or type whatever comes to mind about a particular topic, paying no attention to structure, mechanics, or even logic.

Students generally dislike this technique and believe it is pointless, but it works quite well for many people. At the very least, it briefly silences the cynical and critical voice that haunts many of us as we write—the same voice that tells us we're terrible, our topics are terrible, and that we should just give up.

Collaboration

No, this isn't the cheating form of collaboration. Rather, it is the act of discussing and/or debating an issue with another student, a friend, or a loved one. You'd be surprised how many ideas a simple conversation can generate.

If you happen to be working on a persuasive or argumentative essay, you can even ask the other person to act as an opposing voice and challenge your claims, forcing you to shore up your logic.

Listing

This is just what it sounds like: you sit down and list any and all ideas that come to mind. Think of it as freewriting without all the . . . well . . . writing. Instead of producing chunks of text, you simply focus on the ideas themselves. This may seem appealing to many of you, but many students often miss the momentum they gain with freewriting's *extra* wording.

Outlining

Like some of the other techniques discussed, many of you probably loathe outlines, especially those drawn-out versions that some instructors insist upon. Of course, outlining doesn't need to be extensive to be valuable. Many professional writers, for instance, use quite rough outlines to organize their major points but avoid trying to map out every single supporting idea or piece of evidence.

All in all, outlining is incredibly helpful in producing a logical structure. Rather than wandering through an essay with no real plan, a writer with an outline has a map by which to navigate.

In truth, you can even outline between the first and second drafts (or the second and third, and so forth). Doing so will allow you to step back from the essay itself, recognize any problems in the organization of your points, and make revisions far easier.

There is, of course, something to be said about inspiration, and when inspiration strikes, you should indeed follow its lead. Unfortunately, a person who waits for inspiration to write will produce very little, as it is notoriously unpredictable and unreliable. Ultimately, writing is work, and we must usually approach it as such.

DRAFTING: WHY YOUR ROUGH DRAFT NEEDS COMPANY

At this point, you may be thinking, "I hate rough drafts"; "Rough drafts are a waste of time"; "Rough drafts stifle my creativity, and I avoid them whenever possible." In truth, however, rough drafts are very popular—not because students like doing them, but because that's all most students ever do.

Most novice writers skip the aforementioned prewriting, sit down at their computers, type out whatever pops into their heads, turn in those first drafts, and are somehow shocked at receiving poor grades. Here's the truth: no matter how smart you are, how good at writing you happen to be, or how much you know about a particular topic, you simply cannot create your best work the first time through.

Instructors receive loads of first drafts on a regular basis, all displaying the half-thoughts, tangents, and chaotic structures common in unrevised writing. Many show a great deal of potential, but sadly this is all they show, as the writers consistently fail to develop, refine, and build connections among their ideas.

When looking through your first draft, ask yourself some of the following questions, as addressing several of these issues could vastly improve your paper:

- Did I organize my thoughts well? Does my focus wander or jump around, moving from one idea to the next and then back again? Can I change the placement of a few ideas or paragraphs so that the organization of the paper makes better sense?
- What additional details or examples might I include to develop my ideas further? Are any of my explanations too brief? How could I help readers better understand my points?
- What can I do to show readers how my points and evidence support my thesis statement or connect with one another?
- What other ideas or points can I include that will make my essay more effective, given the audience? Have I met my audience's needs, wants, and expectations? Did I accomplish my writing goals?

Some of you "good" writers out there are perhaps rolling your eyes at this point. After all, you've spent years handing in first drafts and have always received decent grades. Why change what is obviously working?

Put bluntly, there will come a day in your future lives and careers—regardless of your chosen fields—when grades will be a distant memory, when your writing will have an impact far beyond your own successes, and when the "it's good enough" attitude will negatively affect you and many other people. Your employers or employees, your company, your industry, and your reputation will regularly be at stake.

Working hard and improving yourself is a habit, one you need to begin right now. Refine your skills, practice the writing process, and make "your best writing" a habit that will continue for the rest of your life.

JAVIER'S PROGRESS

Javier encountered some problems during the semester, getting fairly low scores on his first two papers. His first essay examined his opinions about the best vacation spot for new college students, and the second tried to tackle drug abuse . . . all of it.

Having grown tired of such grades and his insecurities about the writing process, Javier began to pay closer attention to his instructor's lessons on choosing an appropriate topic, drafting, and revising. Thankfully, his third essay in the class proved much more successful, as it focused on a far more specific issue: *Challenges in Educating Mildly Autistic Preschoolers*.

Javier's third paper also succeeded because he didn't just turn in a rough draft. Instead of surrendering to his usual habit of procrastinating until the last minute, he took his time, used several prewriting techniques, created and revised three entire drafts, and was eventually rewarded for his hard work.

DISCUSSION QUESTIONS

1. Do you complete any prewriting activities or exercises before beginning your papers? If so, which seem to work best for you and why? If not—and be honest—which techniques do you believe will prove most valuable for you in the future?

2. Consider the thoughts that have filled your mind during the last ten minutes. What have you been thinking about, how often does your mind seem to shift direction, and how can the prewriting and drafting techniques discussed in this chapter help you focus while crafting your next paper?

IN-CLASS EXERCISE

The following issues are important but too broad for most essays. Using the techniques discussed in this chapter, narrow the focus of each to a far more manageable and appropriate topic.

1. The American Housing Market Crash
2. Buddhism
3. Modern Educational Challenges
4. The Israeli-Palestinian Conflict
5. The Irish Potato Famine
6. The Evolution of Cancer Treatment
7. Sleep Disorders in Adults
8. Challenges in Senior Care
9. Animal Cruelty in America
10. Violence and Video Games

AT-HOME ASSIGNMENT

- First, write a one-page essay describing one of your great passions—music, sports, art, your family, and so forth. At this stage, pay more attention to the content you decide to include rather than worrying about grammar, punctuation, or even organization.
- Next, reread your original essay and write small comments to yourself in the margins. What ideas seem unclear? What sentences are confusing? Which areas seem to jump around from thought to thought?
- Third, rewrite your original essay, using your comments as a guide. Try to improve the paper's structure, the "sound" of its sentences, the clarity of its ideas, and so on. Once again, don't make the correction of grammar, punctuation, or spelling a focus in this step.
- Fourth, reread and rewrite your revised essay (yet again), correcting any mechanical errors or awkward wording. It's usually helpful to read your text out loud during this step.
- Last, write a short paragraph at the end of your essay describing the improvements you've noticed through your drafts. Is the text better organized? Are the ideas and sentences clearer, more powerful?

Chapter Six

Thesaurus Nightmares: How Trying to Sound Smart Can Make Your Essay Look Stupid

CHUCK'S STORY

Chuck has always been incredibly insecure about his writing skills. However, he's fairly confident that he can fake his way through freshman composition and get on to classes in his major—you know, the ones that *really* matter.

According to Chuck, all one needs is a good thesaurus. Organization, tone, evidence, strategy—all that stuff is nothing compared to the power of big, fancy, multisyllabic words. Those are what make an essay great, and he's quite good at skimming the pages of that thesaurus and locating something truly resplendent, prodigious, scintillating, and coruscating. Awesome, right?

Like the mechanical skills we mentioned in an earlier chapter (punctuation, grammar, spelling, etc.), a strong vocabulary is important in becoming a good writer, but it is often vastly overhyped. Impressive words can be . . . well . . . impressive if used correctly and appropriately for one's particular audience, but all too often the motivations for including such words are painfully transparent and make readers cringe with embarrassment.

Take a look at the following example:

> Welfare reform is absolutely necessary, as the current system is far too wasteful and corrupt. Local and state governments must do more to combat this rampant abuse, both to ensure criminals can no longer take advantage of the system and that families who actually need support receive it.

It's decent, right? Sure, some of the sentences could be stronger, and more details are necessary for true development, but overall the wording is clear and fairly formal. Unfortunately, Chuck believes this kind of writing is too plain, too *ordinary*, to receive a good grade. He therefore decides to use his trusty thesaurus to rewrite it as follows:

> Welfare amelioration is consummately compulsory, as the customary system is far too improvident and iniquitous. Local and state sovereignties must do more to traverse this pandemic delinquency, both to certify that transgressors can no longer finesse the system and that dynasties that indeed necessitate furtherance apprehend it.

If you're looking to aggravate your writing instructor or English teacher, follow Chuck's example, as using wording similar to his will drive even the most patient educator nuts. What was once a decent paragraph with lots of potential has become a tangled mess of incorrectly used words and glittering nonsense.

In trying to "sound smart," Chuck has created a text that is utterly ineffective. While few of you would use a thesaurus to this destructive extent, it is important to realize that even one or two misused words can wreak havoc on one's clarity and credibility.

Always remember that, in addition to a method of thinking and exploring, writing is indeed a means of communication. If you cram your text with gibberish, you're not truly thinking and exploring, and you certainly aren't communicating effectively.

WHAT A THESAURUS DOES AND DOESN'T DO

A thesaurus is indeed a handy tool, as it helps writers avoid repetition by offering us a list of words with *similar* meanings. Having such options is, of course, helpful, as we generally don't want to use the same words over and over again; doing so will irritate readers and make our writing look boring and amateurish. Generally, annoying and boring an audience (especially at the same time) are things to avoid.

Unfortunately, many novice writers fail to realize that the words listed in a thesaurus aren't always true synonyms (different words with the same meaning) and are often just words with *related* meanings. For example, let's say a student has used the word *generous* several times in a paragraph, and she wants to avoid using it yet again—a totally justifiable desire. With nothing good in mind, she goes to her trusty thesaurus, flips through a few pages, and finds the appropriate entry, which looks like this:

Generous
Synonyms: giving, selfless, charitable, philanthropic, fair, liberal

Now, depending on the sentence, a few of these can indeed be used as true synonyms. Let's say the following was her original sentence: "The wealthy widow was very *generous* with her money." Here, she could indeed replace *generous* with *giving* or *charitable*, as they all mean to be selfless in sharing with others: "The wealthy widow was very *charitable* with her money." See? It works just fine.

But these words wouldn't work in all sentences, because the definition of *generous* shifts according to its context. For example, consider the following: "The cafeteria offered a *generous* helping of terrible food." In this case, neither *giving* nor *charitable* would really work, because the meanings aren't the same: "The cafeteria offered a *giving* helping of terrible food." It looks pretty silly, right? Unless you're writing a comedy or trying to be ironic, "silly" is yet another characteristic to avoid.

Of course, Chuck doesn't really concern himself with such issues. Remember, for him the most important qualities of a word are length and complexity. And which word on the list best fits those criteria? *Philanthropic!* Four syllables, thirteen letters—now this is a word that will earn that A, right? So in goes the big, exotic-sounding word: "The cafeteria offered a *philanthropic* helping of terrible food."

Good stuff, yes? Actually . . . no.

Whether it sounds impressive or not, the truth is that being *philanthropic* means being generous in a very specific way, one that doesn't fit this sentence. Indeed, being *philanthropic* means being generous to charity or to the poor. In trying to sound smart, Chuck has revealed himself as a fraud to his readers.

At best, few in his audience will know what the word means and therefore fail to understand his meaning; at worst, some of his readers will recognize the inappropriate word and dismiss Chuck as yet another poser faking his way through a paper.

Do you like posers? Neither do your readers, academic or otherwise.

Even if you do manage to choose a bright-and-shiny word that fits a particular sentence (for example, "The wealthy widow was very *philanthropic* with her money" works just fine), the uncommon and sparkly nature of the word can potentially confuse, distract, and irritate readers.

This isn't to say you should always use mundane vocabulary, but think about your audience before selecting a word based solely on its syllable count.

WHAT YOUR TEACHER ACTUALLY WANTS . . . PROBABLY

The confusion about properly using a thesaurus, and really appropriate wording itself, often stems from a misunderstanding of formal academic style. Haunted by Shakespeare's *thous* and *thees*, or perhaps having endured one too many stilted textbooks, many students think that an appropriate writing style equals over-the-top formality or sentences littered with incomprehensible wording.

In either case, they're wrong. While many writing instructors love Shakespeare, few have a desire to see a student try to mimic him, and even fewer want to find themselves reaching for a dictionary at every third word in an essay. Instead, they want to see a style that reflects your writing goals and audience, one that effectively satisfies the wants, needs, and expectations of your readers.

Whether you realize it or not, you already do this all the time in your daily life. Think about it: How often do you change the way you behave, dress, and speak to meet the wants and expectations of others? For example, do you speak to your grandparents or your boss in the same way you talk with your closest friends?

Imagine sitting down to Thanksgiving dinner with your boyfriend/girlfriend/spouse's family for the first time and letting a few curse words rip. Would they likely invite you back? Don't count it.

Fortunately, most of you out there show an appropriate level of respect for others. In formal academic writing, this is basically what you're doing: you're showing respect for and an awareness of your audience by using wording (also called *diction*) that satisfies expectations. This isn't to say you must write without personality or passion—only that you always need to consider how your wording will likely affect your readers.

Rather than give you a giant list of dos and don'ts, like many other books on writing, the following general suggestions should effectively guide you in making your own decisions about what is and what is not appropriate for your particular writing situation. Remember, these aren't rules; they are guidelines based on writing conventions.

POINT OF VIEW

Few writers new to formal composition think much about point of view, and fewer realize what a dramatic effect it can have on the formality of their writing. Point of view refers to first-, second-, and third-person references—the same three options available to poets and fiction authors. Mastering each of these approaches can be difficult, but it is also vital.

First person is associated with casual writing, as it uses references to the writer him- or herself: "*I* believe everyone can learn to write well" or "*I* think chocolate is the best flavor of ice cream." While referring to yourself can put your audience at ease and help them relate to you as a writer, it's usually too informal for an academic paper because it makes you the text's focus—too many sentences, paragraphs, and claims center on you explicitly. Generally, in formal writing, we want audiences to concentrate on the topic rather than the author.

Second person is also associated with casual writing, as it refers directly to the reader: "*You* can learn to write well" or "*You* are wrong, because strawberry is the best flavor of ice cream." Second person usually works better in an email, personal letter, or text message than in academic composition. This is especially true because we usually know nothing personal about our audience members in that latter situation and can easily offend them.

Imagine seeing the following in a paper you're reading: "Drug abuse is a huge problem in the United States, and you should go to treatment before it ruins your life." Doesn't this sound like an accusation? Is this writer aware that he or she is seemingly accusing a reader of having a drug problem? Difficulties like this can be overcome by heeding the following suggestion: When you don't know your readers personally, avoid addressing them directly through second-person references—unless, of course, you happen to be writing a composition textbook with a casual tone . . . *cough, cough.*

By the way, second person also includes words such as *your, we, us,* and *our.*

An approach using *third-person* perspective is usually best for formal, academic papers, as it avoids referring to either the writer or the reader, making the writing seem more factual and authoritative. Let's look at how a sentence using third person compares to others using first and second person:

First person: I think more should be done to stop child abuse.

Second person: We all know more should be done to stop child abuse.

Third person: More should be done to stop child abuse.

All three of these statements are opinions—good and justifiable opinions, but opinions all the same. Still, the sentence using third person sounds far stronger, as it doesn't include words reminding readers that it is indeed an opinion (e.g., "I think . . ." or "We all know . . ."). In other words, the final claim creates an illusion of objectivity that writers can then support with actual facts and expert quotes. Here's another example:

First person: Family is very important to me.

Second person: Family is very important to our lives.

Third person: Family is very important in the lives of many.

In addition to this sense of objectivity, the lack of personal references creates a distance between the writer and his or her readers, and distance is a significant component of formality.

Think of it this way: Let's say you've been invited to the White House for a state dinner. You buy and wear a great tuxedo or a lovely evening gown, arrive in a limousine, and are then introduced to numerous senators, diplomats, and foreign ministers. In this situation, would it be appropriate to run up and give each person a big old bear hug? When you finally sit down to dinner, would you sip water from your neighbor's glass or ask the head of state seated across from you about his or her personal hygiene habits?

If you answered "yes" to any of the questions above, don't expect that dinner invitation any time soon. Why? Put simply, formal situations call for distance between participants. Rather than hugging complete strangers, we generally shake hands; rather than sharing a glass with someone we've just met or asking deeply personal questions, we maintain a physical and emotional "comfort zone." The same is true in formal academic writing.

This also applies to the use of personal experiences as evidence. Far too many novice writers seem obsessed with themselves and their own lives, and they simply can't wait to share their experiences with readers. In casual conversation or more informal writing genres, personal experiences can indeed be effective pieces of evidence. If you are chatting with a friend about college, and he or she has actually attended a university, his or her tales of dorm life would probably serve as very convincing evidence of what awaits you.

In an academic paper, however, the audience will be far more skeptical. Readers will do one of the following: (1) challenge the accuracy of your experience, (2) see it as just one subjective perspective, or (3) doubt you even had such an experience at all. If they aren't verifiable—as personal experiences usually aren't, by their very nature—few academic readers will find them convincing. In fact, including such personal anecdotes will likely just make them think you're an amateur with nothing important to say.

Generally, academic readers want and expect this same comfortable distance. Instead of focusing on you, they want to concentrate on the claims and information presented in your paper. Instead of relying on your personal experiences as evidence, they want independent and verifiable data.

Finally, rather than be constantly reminded of what you believe, know, see, or think, they want to know why your paper's topic matters to them and their lives.

SLANG AND VAGUE WORDING

An earlier section of this chapter mentioned those long lists found in many writing textbooks of words you should and shouldn't use in academic writing. If you surf the Internet for the differences between formal and informal wording, you'll likely find the same side-by-side comparisons of "good" words and "bad" words in academia.

But rather than focus our attention on particular words here, it's best that you have a strong understanding of the underlying principles. That way, you can choose your own words instead of worrying about memorizing a list.

Many of these no-no words fall into the realm of slang, and not just the kind of slang in bad TV shows or movies. Slang also includes expressions and wording that most of us use regularly. Indeed, many of us use slang so often that we have difficulty determining what does and doesn't qualify. A popular exercise to help students identify such slang asks participants to write a short email to a friend and then analyze the wording therein.

The following is a typical example of those emails. Imagine how a professor would judge such writing in an essay:

> Luis,
> What's up, dude? Sorry I couldn't go the other night, but my stupid car broke down again. Grrrr! Have to wait til payday to get it fixed, but whatever. Hit me up when you get time. Later.

Obviously, this isn't something you would want to submit to your teacher or professor or anyone else you might wish to impress. But what here is specifically slang? "Dude" and "Grrrr" are obvious choices, but keep in mind that slang also includes so-called normal words used in overly casual contexts. For example, there's nothing inherently inappropriate or informal about words like *whatever* and *later*, but the way they're used here makes them so. Would you end a paper with "Later Professor"? Always remember that how you use such words is just as important as their denotative (the definition you'll find in a dictionary) definitions.

If you find yourself still struggling with revising the slang out of your text, the following example may help. The original paragraph is filled with slang, informal sentence structures, first- and second-person references, and other casual wording that would likely put off an academic audience:

> Well, global warming is a big problem, and something totally needs to be done about it. Some people say that it doesn't even exist. Whatever. All you need to do is just look at the weather across the country. Hello! Pretty obvious.

Yes, this may look far more casual than anything you've ever submitted, but many of us still incorporate similar language into our academic essays, albeit to a lesser degree. Next, we'll look at a revised version that attempts to make the paragraph more effective and appropriate for an academic audience (it may help to underline and discuss the changes):

Global warming is an enormous problem, and more must be done to address it. Some people say that it is a myth, but the evidence is clear. All one must do is study current weather reports to recognize this.

VAGUE WORDING

Vague, unclear, and/or nonspecific wording is yet another pillar of ineffective writing in every genre—academic, fiction, business, poetry, and so on. This is why words like *things* and *stuff* so often appear on the previously mentioned academic naughty lists: they're so ambiguous that they could really mean anything and are therefore unhelpful and even frustrating for readers.

Your academic readers will likely be very unforgiving in this regard. They expect you to be an expert on your paper's topic. They're spending valuable time reading your essay, so a lack of specific details and wording will greatly frustrate them. "But I don't know what you mean! Be specific!" they'll cry, hands raised toward the heavens. Maybe they won't be *that* frustrated, but they'll definitely be unhappy.

To avoid causing such irritation, be as accurate and precise as possible in your writing. In fact, let those two words echo in your mind as you craft each sentence—*accurate* and *precise* . . . *accurate* and *precise*.

If the U.S. Department of Education performed a study you use in your paper, state it; don't simply write "the government" or "studies suggest." If you want to support your claims with evidence, use specific facts or quotes. Don't simply tell readers that such evidence exists somewhere out there. And if you find yourself writing *stuff* or *things* a lot, consider writing exactly what you mean instead.

CHUCK'S PROGRESS

It took a month or so for Chuck to realize his thesaurus strategy wasn't working. Fortunately, he gathered enough courage to talk with his instructor after class, who helped him understand and remedy the problem.

Soon, his papers began to improve—first with the absence of overwrought vocabulary, and then in the overall clarity of his sentences. While this didn't make his writing assignments any easier, it did make them much more successful, both in his ability to connect with an audience and in his grades.

Chuck gradually realized that "sounding smart" wasn't nearly as effective or satisfying as showing readers his true intellectual capabilities. Even though he avoided using slang and vague wording, he was eventually able to incorporate his own personality and his own voice into his writing. Such honesty has tremendous power.

Don't neglect that potential. Don't fake your way through a writing assignment and hope the illusion you create will fool your audience. Adopt a style appropriate to your readers, respect them and yourself through the words you choose and use, and, most importantly, write with honesty and passion and power. Such writing has, can, and will continue to change the world.

IN-CLASS EXERCISE

Sometimes creating a more formal text is simply a matter of choosing better wording. As discussed in this chapter, a thesaurus can be helpful for such a task, but relying too much on such a tool can be dangerous.

Ultimately, we want more specific and accurate wording than "fancy" or "sophisticated" language. The list below contains both formal and informal words and phrases. For each informal word or phrase, write down a word or two you might use as a replacement (for example, instead of *big* we might use *great, immense,* or *enormous*).

A lot	Hazardous	Kind of
Really important	Smart	Sad
Hard	Hated	Potential

AT-HOME ASSIGNMENT

The following is an example of very casual writing, the kind that unfortunately often ends up in what should be formal essays. Help the author of this text improve by rewriting it, replacing overly casual wording and/or sentence structure with something more appropriate. Also, feel free to edit the arrangement of the content itself or to add and/or delete sentences as you see fit.

> I think a lot of people forget how important education is and how lucky we all are to get to go to school. Only a couple hundred years ago, like in the 1700s, few kids got the chance. In my research I learned that most were either too poor or had to help take care of family farms or businesses. No thank you! Only rich kids usually got to attend school and study things like history, philosophy, mathematics, and other stuff. Today, all you usually hear is high school and college students whining about hard classes or having to buy their own books. This is silly! We need to appreciate the opportunities we have, because they're good things, not rights.

Chapter Seven

Introductions and Conclusions: Overcoming the Blank Page and the Blinking Cursor

ANDREW'S STORY

Like everyone else in his high school English class, Andrew has endured years of classic novels, writing assignments, and bad cafeteria food. He's also spent plenty of time sitting in front of his computer, staring at blank screens and blinking cursors, struggling to begin his essays.

All of his teachers and textbooks make these introductions sound so easy, and they all seem to give him the same advice: "Whatever you do, for the sake of the world and all humanity, make sure to get the reader interested right from the start." With such advice rattling between his ears, Andrew has grown to despise introductions. After all, how can he possibly make a boring topic immediately interesting? And if it's so easy, why are the beginnings of so many books and articles utterly dull?

Conclusions are also a problem, and yet again all the advice seems the same: restate your main points, your thesis, and then provide a closing. *Snore.* Andrew finds the first two tasks simple enough, boring as they are, and just writes what he's already written in a different way. Unfortunately, the last part—providing a closing statement—always proves difficult, and he's normally so tired when he gets to the conclusion that he often just stops and gives up.

Although he's a decent writer, Andrew rarely gets A's on his papers, and his frustration with introductions and conclusions shares much of the blame. The suggestions for crafting them often sound more like algebraic equations than writing tips, and they rarely help.

INTRODUCTIONS: BEYOND READER INTEREST

First, please understand that there's absolutely nothing wrong with trying to gain reader interest right from the start. It is indeed a worthwhile goal that you should pursue, if possible, but there are several other important goals toward which to strive when crafting a solid introduction (we'll get to those soon enough).

Before doing so, however, it's important to discuss the seldom-mentioned differences between how students and teachers often define *interest*. Most significantly, students often equate *interest* with *entertain* or *excite*. Therefore, when a teacher says, "Make sure you grab the reader's interest," many students hear, "Make sure you entertain and excite your reader."

The instructor, however, is actually more concerned with a student's ability to show readers that the topic is important and worthy of their attention. Entertainment and excitement, as you may have noticed from the usual academic reading assignments, is far from a priority.

With so many students working under this misconception, is it any wonder that many of you have difficulty creating introductions? Most writers, regardless of education, would have a hard time *entertaining* and *exciting* readers in an essay about photosynthesis or the migration habits of African elephants. Like you, they would probably spend an hour staring at their computer screens, wondering how to begin.

Luckily, in academia, we don't need to worry so much about generating that kind of "interest." Instead, we need to focus on providing readers with the information they need to understand our topics and then on convincing them that those same topics are important.

LEADING IN YOUR READER

For a moment, imagine your essay is a beautiful and tidy little home somewhere in suburban America, a home you designed and built yourself. During construction, you made sure the house had a strong foundation, sturdy walls, and durable roof. Working hard and wanting to impress future visitors, you even popped for fine hardwood flooring and a professional paint job for the interior.

But when it came to the home's exterior, you just stopped. You didn't put in a lawn, didn't put in any flowers or trees, and didn't even bother to add a walkway leading from the sidewalk to your front door. Instead, the wonderful little home you worked so hard to build is surrounded by dirt, weeds, and yet more dirt.

When your guests finally arrive for a visit, they drive by the property several times, certain the address must be wrong. Besides, there's no walkway, and none of them are willing to slog through the dirt and weeds. Ultimately, your would-be guests leave disappointed, and all your work means very little.

Without a carefully crafted introduction (the "walkway" that leads the audience from the outside world and their own limited knowledge to your essay's front door), your readers will likely react just like those aforementioned guests: they'll walk away lost, confused, and disappointed.

If you want to avoid this, and you should, the first bricks of that introduction "walkway" you construct should be made of information about the topic's background and/or current social framework. What the heck are those, you ask? Put simply, "background" consists of a topic's significant history—the important elements and events in its past that readers need to know if they are to understand it. Similarly, "social framework" just refers to the current status of or debate about the issue.

Here's an example: Let's say you were assigned to write a paper about the ongoing development of biofuels. As suggested earlier, don't worry about making this topic entertaining or exciting; instead, begin to create that introduction "walkway" by thinking and writing about the topic's background and social framework. Always ask yourself: What does the reader need to know about the topic before getting into the body of my essay? Here are a few important points you find in your research:

- The past developments in biofuel technology have arisen from a wide variety of sciences and industries (background).
- Fuel shortages in recent American history have motivated biofuel research (background).
- Consumption of fossil fuels in countries such as China and India is increasing demand and will continue to drive up prices (context).
- Some experts claim that reliance on foreign oil leaves the United States strategically vulnerable (context).
- There is currently a heated debate concerning biofuels occurring in the United States (context).

Of course, you won't be including all of these points in your introduction; some will be included in the essay's body paragraphs or won't be used at all. Instead, you'll want to choose one or two points that really encapsulate what you plan to communicate in the paper. Will your paper focus on the actual research of biofuels or the current debate about them, or will you pay closer attention to their strategic advantages? And please don't say "all of them," unless you plan on writing a book rather than a paper.

The background and framework points you choose should be fairly general—remember, you want to invite your readers to stroll up the walkway, not throw them down on it—but those points should still reflect the focus of your paper. Again, always keep that previously mentioned guideline in mind: What should the reader know before he or she gets into the body of my essay?

SO WHAT? WHO CARES? WHY DOES THE TOPIC MATTER?

Once you've put in that much-needed walkway, you then must convince readers to actually walk up to the front door of your essay and go on in. To accomplish that, you must persuade them that both your topic and your writing are important to humanity, their communities, or their own personal lives.

Just imagine your reader sitting there with arms crossed and asking, "So what? Why should I care about all this?" You've undoubtedly done the same when beginning a few assigned readings, so don't neglect your audience in that respect.

This may be harder than it seems. Topics are often assigned, and some of you will have difficulty figuring out why they're important at all. Remember, look beyond entertainment and excitement and try to think about the impact or potential impact an issue might have on others. Let's examine a couple of paper topics and see if we can practice this together:

- Challenges in Educating Deaf and Hard-of-Hearing Children
- Earth's Changing Atmosphere

As you can see, there aren't many opportunities here to pursue the entertainment/excitement approach. But considering the topics provided, how are we to answer the "why is this important" question for our readers, especially when many of you are likely wondering the same right now?

If the answer isn't immediately obvious, and often it's not, studying the general academic field(s) or discipline(s) can be an effective starting place. For example, the first topic, *Challenges in Educating Deaf and Hard-of-Hearing Children*, is an issue concerning elementary education—specifically, special education.

Now, ask yourself: Why is special education important? There are, of course, many reasons, not the least of which is that special needs children deserve the same respect and learning opportunities as anyone else. So why, then, would it be important for readers to learn about and help society overcome challenges in educating deaf and hard-of-hearing kids?

Put bluntly, if our society fails to try to surmount those educational obstacles, then all of us collectively abandon the principle of "equality for all." After realizing this, we could then spend a portion of our introduction convincing readers of the same thing.

Let's look at our second possible topic (*Earth's Changing Atmosphere*), and this time we'll break down the process. First, we need to decide this topic's academic field(s) or discipline(s). Here, it's pretty obvious that this is a scientific issue, as chemists, climatologists, and meteorologists could all play a role here. Given that this topic concerns the atmosphere, the last of these choices—meteorology—seems like a good choice.

Now that we have decided upon the topic's academic field, we can study and discover that discipline's importance in the world and to readers. If you've ever been stuck at home because of a snowstorm or seen the devastation tornadoes, hurricanes, or droughts can cause, you're already aware of meteorology's significance. After all, meteorologists study the atmosphere, weather, and climate, and the better such scientists (and the general public) understand these aspects of nature, the safer and more productive our society will be.

This is where our *Earth's Changing Atmosphere* topic comes into play: it's important because weather and climate have a direct and dramatic impact on every individual, every reader. This is a fact that we would want to explain in our introduction.

As is probably apparent by now, this process takes a great deal of practice, but doing so should help give you direction the next time you find yourself struggling to start a new essay.

CONCLUSIONS . . . MORE THAN JUST GOODBYE

After welcoming readers into your essay with a strong introduction, and after educating and inspiring them with the paper's well-developed body paragraphs, the time to say farewell to your *guests* will eventually arise—the conclusion. Unfortunately, far too many novice writers all but ignore this vital component. Whether driven by fatigue, apathy, or a lack of skill, these writers simply abandon their precious readers and leave them lost and confused.

Imagine inviting several new friends on a road trip (yep, it's another analogy). You drive, you talk and laugh, you munch on junk food, and all of you begin to really enjoy one another's company. And then you ditch them in the middle of nowhere, taking the car and the snacks because you're in a hurry to get home and are tired of all the chatter.

That's right—you leave your newfound friends lost and confused and stranded. They'll understand. After all, you put in several hours of driving, so they'll definitely appreciate your desire to get the journey over with. Right?

No?

Well, neither will your readers. Your teacher or instructor, who has likely been ditched more times in essays than he or she can count, certainly won't understand. Despite the usual advice, he or she is probably looking for more in your conclusion than a quick recap of your main points and a hasty *ta-da!*

While the conclusion should indeed emphasize (rather than "repeat") your paper's most significant points, it should do so as a means to an end, not an end in and of itself. To put it another way, the emphasis of your main points should do something more than simply take up space or fulfill a requirement; it should remind readers that your topic is significant to "the bigger picture."

Fortunately, if you did your job in the introduction, you should already have a strong idea of why the topic matters—beyond your ability to get a good grade, of course. Remember our *Challenges of Educating Deaf and Hard-of-Hearing Children* topic? In the introduction, we briefly touched on the issue's larger importance. Once we reach the conclusion, we can elaborate on this significance. In fact, your conclusion is prime territory for driving home the issue's potentially profound and far-reaching impact(s).

For the sake of illustration, let's look at a conclusion that follows the standard advice and contrast it with a stronger version:

> *Standard Version:* We have looked at the many challenges facing those who educate deaf and hard-of-hearing students. First, we examined how deaf and hard-of-hearing children are often discriminated against in classrooms. We then discussed how many teachers struggle in adapting to the special needs of such students. Finally, we looked at ways to overcome these issues.

While it could perhaps be faulted for using second-person references ("we"), this conclusion follows the usual suggestions: it restates a thesis statement and recaps the essay's main points. Snoreworthy, isn't it? In fact, it was probably as boring to write as it is to read. Although mechanically correct, it fails to connect with readers or evoke the critical thought this topic deserves.

Revised Version: While some may contend that today's educational system faces far greater challenges than those associated with deaf and hard-of-hearing children, the treatment and instruction of these special needs students is a fundamental part of America's promise to its citizens. If this nation is to remain true to its creed, if it is to endure as a bastion of liberty and equality in the world, it must recognize and cultivate its deaf and hard-of-hearing youth. Any failure to do so will stand as proof that the American Dream, the vision of so many millions, is dead.

Is it a tad melodramatic? Perhaps. Could it benefit from some changes? Nearly every piece of writing can. Nevertheless, it at least helps readers recognize the connection between this particular topic and a much broader issue: the American Dream.

In illustrating this bigger picture for the audience, the second conclusion reaches out to readers not directly impacted by the essay's topic. They may not know anyone who is deaf or hard of hearing, but those who are American or care about equal rights now have a reason for thinking about your paper long after they've finished it.

BURNOUT

Writing a good conclusion is rarely easy, but there's one more issue we should discuss before . . . concluding. While it goes by many names, "author burnout" is responsible for many bad endings, be they in fiction, business, or academic writing. In the latter case, such burnout usually occurs when students mistakenly believe they must write an essay all in one sitting.

This isn't always just because of procrastination. Students often fear that once they stop writing, they'll never get started again. They therefore refuse to take breaks or try the daily word count discussed in chapter 4, and are ultimately exhausted by the time they reach the conclusion.

Now, the worry many of you have about stopping is definitely natural. This is a challenge that all writers, both novice and professional, must confront. After working hard on a text, we surrender for the night, return to it the next day, and find our minds blank and our fingers sitting idle on the keyboard. Here's another tip: If you return and find that the section upon which you've been working is proving too difficult, begin writing another paragraph or section. That's right—skip that section and come back to it later. There is no rule that demands you write every paragraph in order. Switching it up may help you overcome those episodes of writer's block that make the first words of a new day so difficult.

Once you have momentum, you can always go back and complete the section you skipped. Again, what matters is that you find ways to avoid the exhaustion that cripples your creativity and leaves you saying, "Eh, it's good enough."

ANDREW'S PROGRESS

Obviously, Andrew's difficulties with introductions and conclusions stemmed from misunderstandings concerning purpose and expectation. Once he realized that "entertainment" and "interest" weren't synonymous in academic writing, and that other goals for introductions and conclusions were equally important, everything changed.

More importantly, however, he began to realize that good writing is an art, not a science. It certainly isn't about "filling-in-the-blanks" or depending on "equations." While templates, guidelines, and goal checklists can be helpful—as they're usually based on an understanding of how certain techniques affect audiences—you as a writer must ultimately decide how and when to use them. This includes the techniques and goals discussed in this chapter.

You have a variety of tools and techniques at your disposal, but you must feel your way through every paper you write, relying on your instincts as you mold the words and sentences and paragraphs. Nurturing your artistic sense takes time and practice, so use these tools in that regard, but don't be afraid to develop your writing beyond them.

DISCUSSION QUESTIONS

1. How often do you experience author burnout, and are there specific times when it seems worse than others? Besides the techniques provided in this chapter, what else can you do to combat this precursor to writer's block?
2. In a small group, describe and discuss your difficulties with introductions and/or conclusions—if you have any. What about these parts of an essay makes them so difficult?

IN-CLASS EXERCISE

Choose one of the following topics and write a half-page introduction and a half-page conclusion for it, just as you might if writing an essay about that issue. In the introduction, make sure to emphasize the topic's importance while providing readers with information about its background and/or context. When crafting the conclusion, attempt to show readers the "bigger picture" associated with your chosen issue.

1. The Benefits (or Disadvantages) of High School Sports
2. Internet Gaming Addiction
3. The Battle against Childhood Cancers

Chapter Eight

Flow and Rhythm: What's Missing in Your Writing

KATHY'S STORY

Kathy can't dance. Although a senior in high school and absolutely in love with all kinds of music, she's just never been known for much rhythm or creativity on the dance floor.

The homecoming dance, the winter formal, the prom—Kathy attended all three during her junior year but refused to dance with her partners, certain everyone would mock her offbeat clapping and repetitive gyrations. Even when her friends managed to get her up and moving, her anxiety proved almost paralyzing, and her arms and hips and legs barely budged.

Unfortunately, Kathy's writing shows a similar lack of rhythm and creativity. In her papers, Kathy's sentences are constrained, repetitive, and dull. Rather than displaying variety, passion, and rhythm, her writing just plods from one thought to the next. Each sentence begins the same way, ends up about the same length, and chips away at her English teacher's patience like a tiny hammer and chisel.

Drug abuse is a serious problem. *Tink.* Society needs to do something. *Tink.* Many teens are becoming addicted. *Tink.* Many could even end up in jail. *Tink. Tink.* Many might end up dead. *Tink. Thunk. Crack.*

It isn't that Kathy has nothing interesting to write or that she's neglected her research or prewriting; rather, she simply doesn't understand the musicality inherent in English and all other languages. Although academic writing may lack the rhymes and harmonies of popular music, good prose still relies on the same sense of timing and "flow" that make all your favorite songs so great.

Like many of you, Kathy can improve her writing tremendously by being aware of how her words and sentences "sound" and how they work together to impact the reader. Indeed, this sense of rhythm is often the difference between adequate and really good writing.

THAT ALL-ELUSIVE FLOW

Composition classes often conduct workshops several times in each semester, during which students read and critique the papers of their peers in the hopes of suggesting some ways to improve them. As instructors wander about the class, however, they can expect to hear the same message time and time again, though the words may differ: "I love your paper. It just has such a good flow. Seriously, it flows so well!"

If asked, few of these students could define this magical "flow" that so utterly grips them. If pressed, most suggest it has something to do with the beats of their words and sentences, or how each sentence connects with its neighbors. For example, examine the following paragraphs and decide which is more interesting and pleasant to read. You've already seen the first one:

1. Drug abuse is a serious problem. Society needs to do something. Many teens are becoming addicted. Many could end up in jail. Many might even end up dead.
2. Drug abuse is a serious problem, and society needs to do something. Sadly, many teens are becoming addicted, which can land them in jail. Even worse, many might even end up dead.

The wording in both is pretty much the same, though a few conjunctions (*and, but, so,* etc.) and transitions (*sadly, even worse,* etc.) were added in the second paragraph, as these are excellent methods for developing that all-important flow.

The first paragraph, however, is much more stiff and stuttered—the sentences repeat the same mundane rhythm and display little connection to one another. If you find this kind of writing familiar, pay close attention to the following sections, as learning how to incorporate transitional mechanisms and create sentence variety is vital to making your texts more effective.

TRANSITIONS

Hopefully, most of you have heard the term *transition* at some point in your educational careers. But just in case, let's review a bit: put simply, a transition is a word or phrase that helps readers move from one thought or idea to the next. While there are many kinds of transitions out there to study and use, here we'll focus on those easiest to understand—what we'll dub *transitional mechanisms*.

Now, that may sound quite fancy and difficult, but these are just single words or short phrases tacked on to the beginnings of sentences and/or paragraphs that help readers see how ideas relate. What kinds of words and phrases, you ask? Here are a few of the most common: *for example*; *also*; *in conclusion*; *consequentially*; *first*; *second*; *next*; *ultimately*; *of course*; *lastly*; *finally*; *in other words*; *in fact*; *additionally*; *on the contrary*; *therefore*; *in short*; *put simply*; *as a result*; *unfortunately*; *fortunately*; *certainly*. The examples below show a couple of those words incorporated into actual sentences:

1. Dancing is excellent exercise. *Obviously*, dancing on a regular basis can help a person lose weight and feel better about himself or herself.
2. American musical tastes are often broad but fickle. *Put simply*, a singer or musician can be loved one day and hated the next.

In truth, you undoubtedly use such words and phrases on a daily basis when speaking with others anyway, though you probably don't do so consciously. Think about it. Do you talk like Kathy writes, moving seemingly at random from one topic to another, or do you incorporate little signals that help others keep up with the conversation: *also, of course, as a result, obviously, in fact, ultimately*?

There are dozens of these transitional mechanisms. You must simply learn how to use them with the same fluidity when writing as you do when speaking.

Let's reexamine Kathy's original stiff paragraph to clarify all this. A few transitional mechanisms will be placed among some of the sentence pairs. While reading, think about how these mechanisms function, where they appear, and what they tell readers will come next:

> Drug abuse is a serious problem. *Obviously*, society needs to do something. Many teens are becoming addicted. *As a result*, many could end up in jail. *Sadly*, many might even end up dead.

Did adding a few transitional mechanisms transform the original paragraph into prose rivaling that of Shakespeare? Nope! They did, however, improve the paragraph by changing the sentence rhythms and by helping readers recognize the relationships among those sentences.

In other words, each transition pulled its two respective sentences together like thread woven through a seam, like a magnet between two chunks of steel, and so forth.

Is all this still somewhat fuzzy? That's okay; we'll practice a little more. Here is yet another wooden paragraph that can be improved with transitional mechanisms. In the revision that follows it, a few transitions will be placed among the sentences, all italicized for your convenience. As you read, think about how you would include similar words and phrases in your own papers.

> The popularity of tattooing has grown tremendously in recent years. It has become so popular that traditional stereotypes about tattoos and those who get them are beginning to fade away. Many Americans once believed that tattoos were always associated with criminal behavior, but now they are often admired as artistic expressions. Most Americans now realize that people should be judged by their actions rather than their ink.

The paragraph has a lot of potential, but a few transitional mechanisms can definitely improve it:

> The popularity of tattooing has grown tremendously in recent years. *In fact*, it has become so popular that traditional stereotypes about tattoos and those who get them are beginning to fade away. *For example*, many Americans once believed that tattoos were always associated with criminal behavior, but now they are often admired as artistic expressions. *Ultimately*, most Americans now realize that people should be judged by their actions rather than their ink.

Obviously (see, there's a transition right there), you can and should use transitional mechanisms often in your writing. This isn't to say they must appear at the beginning of every sentence; instead, try to work them in when you feel your paragraphs are getting choppy.

As with every other technique in this book, look upon and use transitional mechanisms as tools to make your writing more effective. Don't just scatter them throughout your paper to satisfy some rule.

SENTENCE VARIETY

Along with transitional mechanisms, paying attention to sentence variety is one of the most effective methods for adding musicality and flow to your writing. Many of you have probably received this advice before, likely scrawled in red ink in the margins of your papers, but this term often confuses many novice writers.

Basically, when a teacher suggests you provide more "sentence variety," he or she is saying that too many of your sentences are of similar length, have similar rhythms, and/or have similar structures.

As we saw early in this chapter, a lack of sentence variety produces writing that is choppy, repetitive, and sometimes utterly mind-numbing. Kathy's original paragraph is a good example of this. To add variety, we must change one or all of the aforementioned elements (length, rhythm, structure).

To avoid boring you, we'll use a new paragraph and give Kathy a brief break—see, adding variety here as well. In the following, remain aware of the lengths, rhythms, and structures of the sentences. In fact, you may wish to read the paragraph out loud, so you can truly hear its plodding nature:

> World War I was horrific. Millions died. New technology was used with deadly effect. It is often overlooked in high schools. Few Americans know much about it. World War II tends to overshadow it. More lessons about World War I should be taught.

Can you imagine reading an entire essay like this? Your English teacher or professor reads such papers on a regular basis.

To improve this paragraph, we're going to incorporate some of those transitional mechanisms we discussed earlier, as well as add variety by changing the structures and rhythms of several sentences. To start, we'll try and unify some of these small sentences into longer compound sentences:

> World War I was horrific, and millions died. New technology was used with deadly effect. Unfortunately, it is often overlooked in high schools. As a result, few Americans know much about it. Also, World War II tends to overshadow it, but more lessons about World War I should be taught.

It's an improvement, to be sure, as the transitional mechanisms and compound sentences have given the text more fluidity. Still, it reads as rather stifled and dull. Perhaps we can play with the sentence structures even further. Taking a lesson from our chapter on development, we'll also build up the paragraph with additional details:

> World War I was horrific. New technology, such as tanks, machine guns, and mustard gas, was used on the battlefield with deadly effect. As a result, millions were killed. Unfortunately, it is often overlooked in high schools, being overshadowed by World War II. Sadly, few Americans know much about "The Great War," and more lessons about it should be offered.

As you can see, the changes in this last paragraph were fairly simple: some of the sentences were left short, others were made longer; transitional mechanisms were added to the beginnings of a few sentences, changing their structures and rhythms; and additional details were added that both changed the beats of several sentences while simultaneously providing readers with more information on the topic.

Some of you out there may be looking on this with skepticism. "How did you know what to leave short and what to lengthen?" you might ask. Or you might wonder how one figures out where and when to change the rhythms or add new details or the transitional mechanisms. Some of you may even be thinking to yourselves, "I can't do this. If I start messing around with the sentences, I'll just make them worse!"

We'll tackle each of these issues one at a time.

How do you know what to leave short and what to lengthen?

Answer: You don't always know, at least not at first. An experienced writer will look at such a passage and know that he or she needs to have a good mix of short and long sentences. With that goal in mind, he or she will try out different variations of each sentence, feeling his or her way through the paragraph.

Admittedly, the initial variations professional writers create are often pretty bad, but that's part of the writing process. You won't usually get it right the first or second time you try a revision, and you may even make it worse, but you must be willing to work through those bad variations to arrive at something worthwhile.

How do you know when to add new details or transitional mechanisms?

Answer: When choosing what details to add and where, simply ask yourself, "Where can I be a little more specific? Also, if I were reading this text, what would I like to know more about?" For instance, the writer of the previous passage decided to include examples of the new technologies used in World War I, probably because he or she knew it would help readers picture these horrific events in their minds.

As for the transitional mechanisms, the author looked at the relationships between each sentence and the one that followed it: Was there a cause-and-effect relationship? Was the second sentence simply adding more information? Did those sentence neighbors express any contradictions? Ask yourselves these same questions when choosing transitional mechanisms, and make sure you get the relationship right.

I can't do this. If I start messing around with the sentences, I'll just make it worse!

Answer: First of all, you *can* do this—absolutely, undoubtedly, as sure as the sun will rise tomorrow. Doing so simply takes practice, just as learning to walk, learning to bicycle, and learning to drive take practice. Secondly, as stated earlier, you must be willing to work the writing process. In other words, you must be willing to make some of your sentences worse (temporarily) in order to eventually make them better.

Sometimes, a good sentence will seemingly pour out of your mind onto the screen. Usually, however, crafting a strong sentence or paragraph or an entire essay will take several tries. Look upon those tries as opportunities for improvement, as do professional writers.

Seriously, if you watched most academics or professionals at work, you'd see them constantly deleting and rewriting material, their expressions changing from disgust to delight after finally getting each and every sentence to "sound" right.

KATHY'S PROGRESS

Well, Kathy still can't dance very well, but she has at least improved the rhythm and flow of her writing a great deal. The journey wasn't an easy one.

Multiple times during the semester, she watched as her classmates breezed through one essay after another, their sentences sophisticated and melodic. Every time she grew frustrated, however, Kathy remembered to be patient with herself and with her writing. She knew that, with time and practice and the right guidance, she could indeed improve—just like all of you can.

You may struggle more than others (or, thankfully, less), but ultimately your efforts will pay off. Imagine how you'll feel when others read your writing and recognize the "music" behind your words. More important, imagine how you'll feel when you begin to recognize it yourself and think, "Hey, this is pretty good!"

DISCUSSION QUESTION

If a new student asked you why sentence rhythm, flow, and variety are important, what would you say? Besides those discussed in this chapter, what other techniques might you use when trying to improve a text's flow?

IN-CLASS EXERCISE

A student has constructed the following paragraph without an awareness of sentence rhythm, flow, and variety. Assist the student, first, by rewriting and improving the paragraph. Once you've finished with the revision, add a brief follow-up paragraph in which you explain your approach and methods for improving the writing. Feel free to add, edit, delete, or rearrange any words and sentences you like.

> Gaming addiction is a serious problem. Many in the United States suffer from this condition. Young people are becoming addicted. Older people are as well. Some spend twelve hours or more playing online games every day. Some even forget to eat or go to work. This resembles drug addiction in many ways. Treatment options should be available. Rehabilitation centers could be created. This would give online gaming addicts the help they need.

AT-HOME ASSIGNMENT

While academic writing and songwriting are quite different genres, we can still benefit from studying the latter. Use the Internet to locate the lyrics of your favorite song, and examine them closely. After doing so, respond to the following questions:

- How do the words and the sentences reflect the music's beat?
- How does the song make use of repetition, emphasis, alliteration (same sound beginning several words in a row), and/or exaggeration to make the song more interesting?
- Have any transitional mechanisms been incorporated among the sentences and phrases? If so, which?
- What can we learn from the characteristics of this song to help us become better formal writers? Be specific and thorough in your response.

Chapter Nine

Argumentative Writing: Finding Your Voice and the Guts to Use It

SCOTT'S STORY

By the time Scott entered college, he'd become pretty good at writing essays. He understood how to conduct research and evaluate sources, he could create varied sentences that displayed a strong and formal style, and he'd all but mastered developing his ideas with details and examples.

But when his college writing instructor asked him to write an argumentative piece, one that "adopted and defended a stance on an important social issue," Scott was stumped. After all, his high school teachers always discouraged opinions in the essays they assigned, telling him time and time again to stick to the facts. "We want objectivity, Scotty," they'd say. "Explain the topic to your readers, but leave your opinions and beliefs out of it."

With little understanding of his new "argumentative" writing goals, Scott wrote his first paper like any other essay: he left out his beliefs and his opinions, and instead provided the audience with pure research. Nothing is better than unadulterated fact, right?

Apparently, his instructor disagreed, as he nearly failed the assignment. Adding further frustration, "adopt and defend a stance"
was scrawled across the top of his paper.

Never one to settle for such a low score, Scott took the opposite
approach to his next paper, filling it with one opinion after another.
It proved fairly easy and therapeutic, actually, as he could simply
state what he believed without worry. Who cared if the audience
agreed or disagreed, or if his ideas offended readers? After all, his
opinions were just his opinions.

Again, his instructor disagreed, and she gave him an equally
terrible grade on the assignment. Scott's desperation grew. Recognizing this, his instructor at last sat down with him, and they discussed the differences between informative and argumentative
writing.

ADOPT, DEFEND, AND CONVINCE

Scott's ignorance concerning the goals of argumentative writing
was at the core of his difficulties. During high school, he'd become
good at writing to educate his readers—the ultimate goal of informative writing—but he'd never been required to convince his readers about much beyond a topic's importance.

Facts were easy; facts were safe. But in argumentative writing,
facts aren't enough, as your primary goal is to convince readers that
your opinions, and the proposals based upon them, are likely right.
To put it another way, in an informative paper, the author acts like a
teacher lecturing in a classroom; in an argumentative essay, the
writer behaves more like a lawyer trying to persuade a jury.

Notice the term used was *lawyer*, not *soapbox preacher* or
heavyweight boxer—your goal is to sway your readers through
logical conclusions based on facts, not to lecture them endlessly or
deliver an intellectual beating. And like a lawyer, every aspect of

your argument—from the facts you present to the examples you provide, to the wording of each and every sentence—should encourage your audience to think and nod and agree.

Repeat the following: *Think. Nod. Agree. Think. Nod. Agree.* If you can guide your readers to do all three, you're doing well.

Of course, if you choose a worthwhile topic (see chapter 5 for tips on choosing an appropriate topic), there will be many voices out there that disagree with your stance. Indeed, if you discover that no one in society disagrees with you, then either your issue isn't appropriate or your stance on it is too neutral.

While you won't have a strong opinion on every issue, neutrality makes for a boring argumentative essay. This isn't to say you must take an extreme stance, but make certain you actually have an opinion with which the audience can agree or disagree.

Instead of lingering in such apathy or shying away from heated discussions, embrace the dialog that controversial issues can generate. Real democracy, and perhaps even the progression of humanity itself, depends upon the thoughts of everyday citizens and the discussions that take place among them. Consider the following argumentative stances, all of which had plenty of opponents at various times in history:

• A king or queen is subject to the law and to the will of those he or she governs.
• The enslavement of any individual is both immoral and absurd.
• Women are the intellectual, social, and political equals of men.

Obviously, such conversations aren't always comfortable or easy, and your voice alone may not enact sweeping change, but you can at least take part in the discussions and decisions that affect us all. Such discussion and decisions are absolutely necessary, as should be plain from the previous examples.

Ultimately, you deserve to be heard, but you must also learn to be effective in how you present your voice so others will listen.

HOW IT'S DONE: THE THESIS STATEMENT

At the beginning of each semester, when students are asked about their difficulties in writing, creating thesis statements ranks right up there with grammar and citations. A large percentage of students absolutely despise these rhetorical bogeymen, but perhaps those feelings are understandable. Thesis statements are, after all, a central focus of many writing classes, and yet confusion about these little terrors abounds.

In truth, there's absolutely nothing to fear. Put simply, a thesis statement in argumentative writing is just a sentence or two that announces a central claim, usually early in your paper. What do you want readers to agree with after they finish the essay, and why should they do so? Your thesis should clearly and concisely answer this question.

Yep. That's it. In essence, this is all a thesis statement does, but clearly communicating your argument's core claim is still of utmost importance—the audience can't and won't agree if they're confused about what you're arguing. Students usually have difficulties with these concise declarations for various reasons. See if any of these items strike you as familiar:

- *Lack of focus:* Either you've chosen an issue that's too broad or you're not certain of the precise topic. Creating a thesis statement without a clear focus is like venturing into the wilderness without a map and compass: you'll just end up wandering in circles.
- *Lack of opinion/stance:* You forget or are unwilling to include an actual opinion or proposal (what you think should be done) in your thesis. As you can imagine, it's hard to write an effective argumentative paper without incorporating an actual argument.

Remember, your goal isn't to remain neutral or give attention to all sides of an issue; you're not a journalist. Instead, your goal is to convince readers to agree with you.

- *Runaway finger syndrome:* Your thesis statement never seems to end, running a paragraph or more. When you become more advanced in your skills, you can certainly imply your thesis rather than state it explicitly, but master the fundamentals first.

 Keep your thesis fairly brief. It doesn't always need to be only one sentence long (unless your teacher says so, in which case you should heed his or her advice/requirements), but definitely keep it under three lines or so.

- *Word tangles:* Sometimes, a student simply tries too hard in a thesis statement, being more concerned with sounding profound or following a template (claim plus three supporting details) than with communicating clearly. In these cases, the wording often gets tangled, confusing, and/or redundant. If you find yourself doing this, avoid trying to say too much in a single sentence. It's perfectly fine to add a follow-up statement.

As with your introductions and conclusions, you'll probably have better results focusing on goals rather than on fill-in-the-blank templates. Besides, as with everything else in writing, thinking about and remaining aware of what you're doing is tremendously important. So what are the goals of a thesis statement? Here are a few of the big ones:

1. Clearly communicate your central claim and overall argument to readers.
2. Provide at least some support for that claim, usually in the form of a well-reasoned interpretation of your paper's evidence.
3. Provide a context for your stance: How does it fit into the overall debate (optional)?

Weak and ineffective thesis statements fail to achieve one or all of these goals. Strong and effective theses, however, accomplish at least two of them in a concise and powerful fashion.

Like every other writing skill, learning to produce the latter kind of thesis takes time and practice, so be patient with yourself; in addition, consider revising your thesis statements several times, even after you've finished a paper. Commonly, you will think about and discover new concepts during the drafting phase, and the ultimate direction of your essay may shift. Your thesis should always reflect that new direction.

Let's look at a few samples to illustrate how different theses achieve or fail to achieve the aforementioned goals. Below, you'll see pairs of thesis statements, each containing one weak and one strong example. Examine them closely, read the included explanations, and try to develop a sense of what makes them effective or ineffective.

1. Welfare reform is a very controversial issue today, but few people understand the issue in depth. (weak)
2. Welfare reform is an absolute necessity, as fraud and corruption plague the system and prevent truly needy families from receiving the help they deserve. (strong)

Explanation: Obviously, the first example fails to communicate an actual argument, offering a fairly obvious fact in its place. Remember, your thesis should express an opinion, as in the second example; it shouldn't just state a fact.

1. Child abuse is wrong, and too many children suffer under abusive parents. (weak)
2. The federal government should impose far longer sentences on abusive parents. Doing so will discourage such destructive behavior and ultimately protect millions of otherwise vulnerable children. (strong)

Explanation: While the first statement does indeed express an opinion, it isn't one with which many reasonable readers would disagree. How many readers out there would claim child abuse is good and just? Probably few, if any. Instead, it's more effective and useful to argue a claim that someone might oppose. In regard to the second example, for instance, someone might disagree by referring to overcrowding in prisons or false accusations by teens.

Most important, always remember that the thesis statement is a tool for you and your readers, a method for ensuring your audience understands your argument and thus is capable of agreeing with it.

All too often, students see these declarations as simple rules, as requirements they must fulfill if they want a decent grade. But, as mentioned several times in this book, don't develop your skills just because someone says you must; instead, learn to create better theses because doing so will greatly improve your ability to connect with an audience and to enhance a reader's understanding of what you're trying to say.

THE WEEPY, THE DREAMY, THE ANGRY, AND THE SCREAM-Y

Many of you out there probably believe that emotion is unnecessary and even inappropriate in writing, at least in any genre outside of fiction or poetry. Emotion belongs in soap operas but never in formal writing, correct?

Baloney! While you do indeed want to maintain control of your feelings in formal and academic writing (otherwise, you'll appear melodramatic or berserk to readers), don't ignore emotions altogether. In fact, if you can understand and then evoke your readers' emotions, you're much more likely to succeed in your writing goals.

Television commercials provide excellent examples of the effectiveness of emotional appeals in convincing an audience of something (those marketing people really know their stuff, don't they?). Think for a moment about the commercials you see on a daily basis: How many try to affect you on an emotional level? How many include images that attempt to make you sad or hopeful, angry or afraid?

It's no accident. We humans are emotional beings, and emotional appeals often slip right past our rational defenses—for good and for bad—and marketers know this. Politicians, teachers, dictators, parents, public relations spokespeople, real estate agents, writers, you: almost all of us try to affect others emotionally on a regular basis.

While such manipulation can and has been used for evil, there's nothing inherently immoral about it. It's simply part of being an effective communicator and a member of any society. And if you wish to become a strong argumentative writer, you'll need to master emotional appeals yourself.

When crafting your argumentative essay, ask yourself some of the following questions, as they're designed to get you thinking about how to connect emotionally with your audience and thus increase your paper's potency. Always remember, however, that there is often a fine line between trying to spur emotions in your readers and turning your essay into a melodramatic mess.

1. What does my audience likely value? What do my readers think is important, and how can I emphasize its connection to my topic?
2. What aspect of my topic seems especially sad, inspiring, irritating, or scary? How can I help readers recognize this?
3. Where in my essay can I use an example that paints a picture in readers' minds? What can I describe that will affect them emotionally?

Always consider such questions when writing essays about inherently emotional issues. For instance, consider a topic that has the power to touch even the most objective and rational readers— the abuse and neglect of senior citizens.

As an illustration, let's say you're writing an essay in which you argue that state governments should do more to protect seniors from potential abuse, especially in rest homes and hospice centers. Taking a tip from an earlier chapter, you offer details to develop your readers' understanding of the problem, but all you come up with is the following paragraph:

> While most people agree that the prevention of elderly abuse and neglect should be a national priority, too little is being done to protect vulnerable seniors. Despite the passage of many laws meant to stop such abuse, reports of filthy living conditions persist.

While the writer offers some decent details and maintains a formal style, she has still missed out on a tremendous rhetorical opportunity by ignoring the topic's built-in emotional potential.

We naturally want to be subtle in our efforts to evoke those feelings, and therefore we need to tread carefully. In the following revision, we'll simply add a detail or two that places an emotionally evocative image in readers' minds:

> While most people agree that the prevention of elderly abuse and neglect should be a national priority, too little is being done to protect vulnerable seniors. Too often, families visit their loved ones in retirement homes and hospices only to find them covered in bedsores, sleeping in urine-soaked beds, and starving after days without food. Traumatized, some can no longer speak. Others can do little more than weep and beg for rescue.

Now, would you want to include such details for every claim that you argue? That's doubtful. The choice is, of course, yours to make, but always keep your audience in mind. Offer too few emotional appeals and you might miss out on an effective strategy and fall short of your goals; offer too many, and you may drive your readers away.

SCOTT'S PROGRESS

Scott has come a long way in his understanding of argumentative writing, its goals, and how to reach them. In fact, his recent papers have received top marks, as they displayed both well-reasoned and well-defended claims, all augmented with powerful emotional appeals and refutations of opposing voices.

In addition to his improving grades, Scott's grasp of argumentative writing forced him to take a closer look at his own beliefs—which may be even more important. It's easy to simply have opinions, but the process of explaining and justifying them to others often brings about renewed perspective. We begin to ask ourselves questions, to explore doubts, to consider other ideas and approaches, and to make conscious and logical decisions about what we believe, what we don't, and what others say we should.

DISCUSSION QUESTIONS

1. Identify and describe a controversial social or academic issue that you believe is very important in today's world. Why do you think this issue is so significant, what are your opinions concerning it, and how do those opinions conflict with the thoughts and claims of others? Be specific and thorough.

2. How much and in what ways do your emotions influence your decisions and beliefs? Are there particular subjects that seem to intensify your emotional responses more than others?

IN-CLASS EXERCISE

Find a partner and select one of the following controversial issues to discuss, preferably one about which you disagree. On separate sheets of paper, each of you must then write down a declaration that states your opinion about the issue and lists four or five reasons why you hold that belief. This may take some time, so be patient with yourselves—but make sure to be honest. Here are the possible topics in question form:

- Is climate change heavily influenced by human technology, transportation, and/or industry?
- Should those who receive government assistance (food stamps, welfare, etc.) be required to take drug tests?
- Should summer vacation be eliminated and replaced with an additional semester?
- Should all Americans, at age eighteen, be required to spend two years in either the military or a civil service organization?

After you've completed the outlines, have a casual debate about the issue between yourselves. As in a formal argumentative essay, the goal here is to convince your partner to agree with your stance—not simply to state your opinion. Offer your points, listen to your partner's claims, refute one another, and so on.

In all likelihood, neither of you will have succeeded in changing the other's mind. This doesn't make the debate a failure, however, as you've begun a conversation about an important issue.

Following your debate, discontinue the attack on one another's claims, and instead try to find common ground among them. Are there any points upon which you can agree? Is a compromise possible? What valuable information or approaches can you glean from one another's arguments?

AT-HOME ASSIGNMENT

Use the Internet to research a famous political speech from history (from ancient Rome to the twenty-first century). Examine how the speaker attempts to convince his or her audiences of a particular claim. For example, after the bombing of Pearl Harbor on December 7, 1941, how did President Roosevelt convince Congress and the nation to declare war on the Japanese empire? What techniques did he use? To what emotions did he appeal?

Choose an era and speech that interests you, and write a one-page analysis of the speaker's techniques and your perceptions of his or her effectiveness.

Conclusion: Why Writing Matters . . . and Yes . . . It Does

Yes, writing matters. Reading and thinking also matter, and all three are indelibly tied to one another. Few of you out there likely intend to become professional writers, and just as few probably want to be English teachers, but in the end that's not important. The necessity of these skills is universal, transcending career choices and academic disciplines.

Indeed, most students regard English and composition classes, both in high school and college, as mere hoops through which they must leap—chores, really. Hopefully, however, the conversation here has encouraged you to adopt a different perspective, one that recognizes the value of strong writing skills both in the classroom and beyond.

And the same goes for those of you already out of school. Even in the business world, there are enormous numbers of professionals who once looked upon writing as a necessary evil for letters to clients, reports, and advertising but later deeply regretted their lack of skill in expressing themselves.

Like a lot of them, many of us spend our young professional lives so focused on careers and salaries that we all but ignore our artistic selves, as if that aspect of ourselves is somehow silly and pointless. Nonsense! Exploring humanity through artistic endeavors like writing is never a waste of time. Please, never forget that.

Remember, writing is far more than simply placing lines and dots across a page, just as flying an airplane is more than just pressing buttons on a control panel. Writing is a powerful collection of skills and techniques that enable us to think, to explore, to connect, and to communicate. Perhaps more than any other art form, writing has impelled humanity's social and moral evolution, and it will continue to act as the thread that binds together our shared past, present, and future.

In the end, writing well isn't about nouns and verbs, essays dripping red with ink, or English teachers demanding better thesis statements. It is rather about confronting and transcending confusion, fear, and ignorance. It is about bridging, even if just temporarily, that which separates and divides us. Indeed, writing is about being a member of and a contributor to humanity itself.

So grab a pen, a keyboard, or an antique typewriter (if you're the dramatic sort).

Go explore. Go connect.

Go contribute.

CPSIA information can be obtained at www.ICGtesting.com
Printed in the USA
BVOW031306300412

288920BV00005B/1/P